STAFFLESS

FRONT DESK SOLUTIONS FOR SOLO PRACTITIONERS

DR. JODI DINNERMAN

Disclaimer.

Although the author has made every effort to ensure that the information in this book was correct at press time, they do not assume and hereby disclaim any liability to any party for any loss, damage, or disruption caused by errors or omissions, whether such errors or omissions result from negligence, accident, or any other cause.

This book details the author's personal experiences with and opinions about practice management. The author is providing this book and its contents on an "as is" basis and make no representations or warranties of any kind with respect to this book or its contents.

Furthermore, the author disclaims all such representations and warranties, including for example warranties of merchantability and healthcare for a particular purpose. In addition, the author does not represent or warrant that the information accessible via this book is accurate, complete or current.

The statements made about services are not intended to educate you regarding how to diagnose, treat, cure, or prevent any condition or disease. Please consult with your professional board and regulatory commissions regarding the suggestions and recommendations made in this book.

It is imminent that you abide by your local and national requirements and guidelines as it pertains to client privacy, laws, and allowances. Except as specifically stated in this book, the author, nor any authors, contributors, or other representatives will be liable for damages arising out of or in connection with the use of this book.

This is a comprehensive limitation of liability that applies to all damages of any kind, including (without limitation) compensatory; direct, indirect or consequential damages; loss of data, income or profit; loss of or damage to property and claims of third parties. You understand that this book is not intended as a substitute for your requirements and responsibilities as a licensed healthcare practitioner.

Nothing lights my world up more than being able to deliver real-deal support and direction to wellness practitioners all over the world. Learn about my shenanigans and all of my offers in my wildly wonderful Facebook™ Group. www.facebook.com/groups/stafflesspractice.

Hi, I'm Dr. Jodi Dinnerman.

One thing I know for sure is that there is a divine order to all of this. The people we meet, the paths we cross, the lessons we learn — it all has a purpose. Let me share a bit about who I am to better understand the purpose of this book.

First and foremost, I am a mom. I love nothing more than hanging with my boys — two teenagers who will for sure be appalled when they see this reference (especially with my cool terminology). The challenging balance of figuring out the *mom-thing*, while running a busy practice has been a great one.

My husband has been my best friend and life partner since the day I laid eyes on him, over 25 years ago. We have it good over here. We work hard, rest hard, and play hard.

I have parts of me that are lazy, some that are over-driven, some that are obsessive, and some that are disconnected. They all count, and their marriage is what makes me who I am.

I am deeply committed to the philosophy, science, and art of chiropracTIC. It keeps me straight and on point, daily. I learned confidence in craft from my mentor, Dr. Sue Brown, whom I owe the inspiration of this book to.

I am forever grateful to the people in my life who have made me laugh so hard that I couldn't breathe, there have been a few of you. I am just as grateful to the people who have given me the hard-to-swallow lessons — *GODspeed*.

The discovery of SEWP School and the students I have the privilege to serve has made every lesson learned and heartache felt worth it. Thank you for choosing me and my program.

My birth-family is a unique one — I take pride in being the product of two compulsive business starters, three brothers, and a sister, each with the gift of continuous surprise and unpredictability. I have learned so much from each of you.

I serve family chiropractic care in Clinton and Princeton, NJ. I truly adore the people I serve. Discovery of the flow and balance for my adjusting room has been the ultimate teacher, developing and shape-shifting the concepts of this book.

I am completely committed to the path of my future. I will continue to let the AHA moments of life shake me to my core — to becoming a better version of who I am meant to be. The longer I journey through this life the more my heart fills with gratitude.

I pinch myself often.
Ouch — there I go again.

Forward by Amy J. Burke, D.C.

I am so excited for you to read this book. It is going to change your life. STAFFLESS is going to give you hours of time that you can CHOOSE how to spend rather than attempting to manage an office staff who simply cannot love your practice in the same way you do.

Everyone has issues, everyone is imperfectly perfect, everyone has different skill sets and strengths. Is it really your job to figure out all the pieces of that puzzle? There is a way to set up your practice so that you can manage it all. Dr. Jodi Dinnerman has taken the guesswork out of creating systems that can make your solo practitioner office soar.

I have witnessed brilliant, talented, dedicated, successful practitioners spend tens of thousands of dollars a year in order to figure out how to get their staff on board in making their dream office a reality. I have attended retreats that were designed to offer a respite to professionals drained from the tremendous work they do. Do you know what they talked about?

Not the miracles they witnessed daily in practice, that was the EASY part of their day. In the midst of a mountain paradise, a swim in the sea, an incredible meal amongst colleagues, managing people, personalities, and creating a compensation package that was fair to everyone was the number one topic of conversation. I was blown away by the time, effort and RESOURCES that managing people requires. None of this is taught in school.

Many offices that welcome interns or associates are dysfunctional themselves and so teach you what you want to avoid, but don't model what you want to create. Enter Dr. Jodi Dinnerman. She has gone through all the painful, uncomfortable, expensive steps of having a successful practice that required too much effort for all of the the wrong reasons.

Dr. Jodi has put it all together this book for you so that you can learn from her process and start immediately to create a practice environment that will support you, not drain you.

My own staffless practice was born from necessity. I had a 256 square foot office in Manhattan and five chiropractic adjusting tables. I simply didn't have room for another person in my space. I did it all, and I LOVED it.

I came up with creative solutions to address the missing person.

I also wasted ZERO energy on things that I am not good at and didn't care to learn about: hiring, firing, delegating, managing expectations, staff meetings, handbooks, labor laws.

I invested my time and money on what I loved, connecting with the people in my practice. Over twenty years have passed and the technology has beautifully evolved to meet our needs as solo practitioners, allowing us to focus on the aspects of practice we love the most: serving the people who seek our care.

In this book, Dr. Jodi covers exactly what strategies you need, and how to set it up to avoid wasting time on things that are distractions, things that don't add to your bottom line.

If you are spending your precious free time figuring out how you can better manage the personalities in your office, if you are spending thousands of dollars a year in coaching services that help you better train, sculpt, and script your staff, if you are drained at the end of your day because you have to add time to deal with issues in the office that are not yours, this book is the greatest gift you can give to yourself this year.

Amy J. Burke, D.C.
Venice, Italy

Dedication.

Words can't express…
Jim, my rock.
Kai, my teacher.
Quinn, my joy.
Maria, my wind.
Mom, my mirror.
Sue, my interpreter.

In constant gratitude to the clients I serve, you have given me the ultimate learning platform.

All good things to those who have contributed to my lessons learned and experience earned.

Introduction.

This book is an introduction to the building blocks of the Staffless Practice Success System — a three-pillar network of copy-and-paste tools for realizing practice success, without staff. It's a simple taste test taken from the elaborate (and delicious) menu of SEWP School — the online finishing school for the Staffless Entrepreneurial Wellness Practitioner.

The pieces included in this book took countless, thought-out hours to organize in such a way as to not overwhelm you, but also provide you with practical, implementable resources.

I broke this book into very clear divisions:
- A deep dive into how and why STAFFLESS came to be, where my journey took me to end up here, in this moment, offering you these lessons.
- The essential tools for preparing for practice success as a Staffless Practitioner, tools that when implemented correctly, will completely shift and maximize your practice efforts.
- My streamlined client communication strategies which make running a practice without staff completely possible. Real-deal organization systems that create space and order for the Staffless Practitioner.

This book is not for the practitioner who is looking for a quick fix.

Doesn't exist.

Sorry.

The perfect app, or course, or tech to make practice-building and maintaining simple is just not a thing. Period. I learned that the hard way. After hundreds of thousands of dollars spent on the *this is going to do it* programs, I saw the very thick forest through a shit-ton of trees.

If you are wanting to streamline your client communications and find the balance between service, abundance, hard work, fun, and success... read on.

This book is for the practitioner who does not want staff for whatever reason, and wants to learn how to do it solo. On the other hand, it is also for the practitioner who does have staff, and wants to streamline their team roles in order to truly push each team members' talents forward.

I totally appreciate that there are many practices out there who have staff, and do it right. You rock, just not my world. I appreciate your ways and honor your systems. I also recognize that there are many, like me, who need to and want to fly solo.

So, dive in. Red-pen, dog-ear, and highlight the juice out of each relevant bite in this book. Make it count, make it a game-changer.

Dr. Jodi Dinnerman

Contents.

The four promises.

You did it. You got here. I'm about to share some secrets with you that could very potentially rock your practice experience, expand your practice palate in ways you never knew possible, and reignite the fire in your belly to serve like never before. Let's start with a few things to consider before you turn the pages of this book.

Chances are you want to run a staffless practice, or a practice with staff that only does what they are truly great at doing. You need to get all of the things to all of the people, at all of the right times, and it seems like a huge thing. Like, huge.

Listen — been there, done that.

I have four promises to make to you. Ready?

First, yes you can.
If I can do it, anybody can do it. I come from a background of needing to study twice as hard as my classmates (through ten years of college), being labeled with every learning disability out there, and living in a world of total crisis all the time. I always knew I had it in me to do great things, but I never knew how to find the vehicles through which to reach that greatness. I still search, screw up, clean up, love up, and repeat — like, daily.

Second. Struggle is motivation fuel.
Struggle has always been my motivation — falling down, getting back up, brushing off the hurt, and figuring out a solution to prevent it from happening again. That's how I have created these systems. I have done all of the falling necessary for you, my reader.

I am giving you all of my automation tools to throw into the mix, so that while you are busy creating and living the life of your dreams, your practice is running like a well-oiled machine. You really can be on the baseball field with your kid, or the gym floor with your pals, or on a very fancy beach chair in Hawaii, while your practice is running itself in the background. Follow my lead. I will get you there.

Third. Service is the name of the game.
The truth is that your path as a practitioner is NOT about you, your story, and your gains. Ever.

It is about service. I would just about bet my last chocolate bar on the fact that if you picked this book of all of the books out there, you are ready for the lessons it offers. Serve the people great care. Period. The more people you serve, the more good you are creating. And the world needs more good, like yesterday!

Fourth and final. If you listen for your calling, you will hear it.
I did not become a family chiropractor because I

wanted to get rich, or have a big house, or a fancy car. I was grabbed and shaken to my core with my calling — to live a life of serving LOVE through chiropractic.

Love; it wins every time. Love can make or break your experience as a practitioner. If you don't love what you do, and love why you do it, it may be time to change a thing or two.

I still listen, I still hear my calling loud and clear. I still love hard. When was the last time you listened, you got quiet and still enough to hear your calling, and felt true love for your practice?

Lean in, listen up.

Let it grab you by the ass, shake you up in such a way that you don't know what hit you, and set you on a path of service, a path of mastery.

Heads up, if you have not been shaken, chances are it's coming.

Your calling awaits you.

1
THE STRUGGLE IS REAL

It got so bad, I went staffless.

My personal ways make being a boss messy. I fall in love with people. I give too much, and it ends up being completely overwhelming for all involved.

A wise friend told me when it comes to staff, be friendly, not friends. I don't know how to do that. My cut is to love hard. At this stage of the game, learning to love less takes a ton of effort.

And then there is my vision, my personal attachment to the philosophy of what I do.

I want my practice vision to touch every single experience my clients have in my office. And no matter what I threw in the team training recipe, the vision got blurred, sometimes in small ways, sometimes big. But blurred was not working for me.

I really wanted to figure this staff thing out. I took the seminars and hired the coaches and read the books, only to end up in the same place over and over. Old dog, new tricks. Ruff.

Part of growing up in practice is knowing what your weaknesses are (which is always where your gifts come from) and how to cater to them. My weakness? Managing others. I am not cut out for it. I don't have the patience or the perspective. And learning that — like, really learning it — was tough.

I grew tired of the long nights in the office, clearing up drama and headaches, getting home late. There were evenings that I would get home at 9PM because a system or process in the office got confused or miscommunicated with a team member.

I started missing my family dinners and bedtime prep with my kids. Sure, my boundaries could have been cleaner and clearer.

I could have had a hard stop at 6PM and out the door by 6:30, but my practice needed me.

And you know what? So did my kids. Oh, my kids. I blinked, and they were taller than me. It's gone. And here I am, wishing I did it differently all those years ago.

My practice was feeling like a job, a job that was taking me away from my family and the freedoms that I longed for. I was a mess. I couldn't figure it out. I wanted to succeed. I knew I could do it.

I was once told that when tragedy and crisis happen, the cream rises to the top. I get it. I like cream. Here we go.

When I had finally had enough of the lessons, the heartache, the time/money spent and the yearning to be home more, I was ready for change. I had to create a solution for myself to finally enjoy practice again, and for me, that meant without staff. I knew I could do it. So, I started with a list.

The system I needed was born.
I made a list of every system my staff was running that needed to be replaced with automation. Messages, billing, scheduling, rescheduling, new client care, office care, etc. They all needed solutions. One by one, I created them.

The birth of the Staffless Practice Success System was happening. I can't say it was easy to figure out or didn't take hard work, but I pulled up my sleeves and did it. I was on a freedom mission. I would plan and implement a system for this and that, try it on, massage it until it was just right, then move on to the next. I didn't totally know what I was doing while I was doing it, but I figured it out, piece by piece.

I learned how to turn my office phone into a client directory, providing my callers the solutions they were seeking without dropping the message of my vision. I learned how to create emails that were useful and relevant to the people receiving them, that went out when they needed to, without me doing a thing. I learned how to create the checklists to remind me of what needed to get done, when it needed to get done.

I looked for feedback from by-the-way comments my practice members would make. I would hear *I love how you do this scheduling thing*, and *your phone system is so convenient and easy to follow*. Yes! Can you imagine how great that felt?

I could feel the flow in my schedule balance, the energy in my body increase, and freedom in my heart build.

It worked. It really did.

My schedule was full. My time was organized. My payroll was zero. My clients were happy. My kids had their mom back.

The Staffless Practice Success System was running the show for this very busy, fun-loving, mission-driven chiropractic Mama.

Fast forward to the spring of 2020. The world changed overnight. The way we practice had to change, too. My colleagues were losing their teams left and right. No one wanted to come in to the office. No one felt safe. Running a staffless practice became the new way of doing things.

Many of my friends in practice had watched my transition to creating and implementing the Staffless Practice Success System. They started to lean on me to learn the way.

I shared my systems with them. I watched them implement what are now the three pillars of the Staffless Practice Success System, and it worked for them too. In fact, it worked so well, that many of them never went back to having staff on site. Like me, they found that running a practice without staff created more joy, less stress, and more income for their practice.

Justine, the dentist with a vision.

Justine is a unique, creative, force-to-be-reckoned with dentist. She truly believes in what she does and how she wants to do it but her ways are just not working. She has been in practice for five years and keeps hitting the same walls. Every time she hits them, she hits harder, and it hurts more. Her number one pain point is managing staff.

When she was a little kid, she got inspired, like really inspired, by her very cool, earthy, hippy-happy dentist. Dr. Jean had a home-practice that smelled like cookies and felt like a warm blanket.

She had four very sweet kids whom she was home-schooling, and they were always hanging out in the office, engaging with the clients, making each person feel right at home. There was no staff in the office, just her and her family and her dog, Bart.

It took two visits with this amazing mentor to set Justine on a path of saving money and planning success for a perfect family dentistry practice of her own.

And here she is, 25 years later. Five years in practice, and lost. Where did things get messed up? How did she get here? She has a team who doesn't get her vision, doesn't even like working for her.

A huge part of the practice's income goes to their payroll, not to mention the amount of time she puts into managing and training them. No matter how hard she tries and how many different ways she tries it, she cannot get it right with her staff.

Justine didn't go to school and spend hundreds of thousands of dollars to become a team manager. She had a calling, dammit! She loves her work, and she just wants to focus on serving her clients. She didn't get trained to run team meetings or manage employee issues. The last thing in the world that she wants is to hurt somebody or to make their job difficult, but what's happening now is not working.

The problem; wrong people in the wrong positions. They are sweet and kind and really nice people, and all, but not into it. Not into it the way that she needs them to be. They come in late, if they come in at all. They are attached to their phones, disconnected from the patients, and just don't seem to respect the practice. They have very little desire to make it happen with Justine, to see her practice really succeed. They are there for a part-time job, and their part-time job is being served with a part-time attitude.

Justine spends a good deal of her non-client time at the office creating, reviewing, and checking off employee to do lists.

As the practice changes and evolves, and the needs of the clients change, the team roles change too. The checklists change, the training changes, and it's just too much to keep up with.

She comes to the office every Monday ready to rock and roll, with new ideas and new strategies, only to be greeted with blank stares and deep sighs.

She is getting to the point of giving up. She wants to quit. She is either going to shift things, like big time, or leave the practice all together.

Justine can't help but fantasize about the setup in Dr. Jean's office all of those years back.

Welcoming. No staff. Calm. Happy. Cookies and warm blanket. She longed for it. She longed for flow and calm and good. Her staff and training and jobs were in the way. In her way. But how could she change it?

Could she replace her current staff and what they do, or don't do, with automated systems, and maybe even have a virtual assistant to do odd jobs that she really doesn't want to do?

The answer is yes! Yes Justine!

With the right tools and systems, you and countless practitioners who don't want staff, can spend much less time on their practice and so much more time in it, truly practicing in joy.

I make a miserable manager.

One of the gifts that comes with being a seasoned practice owner is knowing (all too well) what my growth roadblocks are. Managing staff is at the top of the list. My problem — the amount of energy and time it takes me to balance the hats that need to be worn when I am in the office. It's nearly impossible.

One hat for giving and serving and being all heart. One hat for having a business sense of who needs what, when.

Throwing another hat in the mix to manage staff has always been too much. Too many hats for this head.

The hiring trap.
It can be tough. We set our practice up, get it running, and most practitioners usually default to the next step of hiring staff. Hand over this paperwork and those phone calls. Make the due diligence of everyday practice someone else's problem.

But the truth of the matter is, unless we have a background in managing staff, we usually end up hiring wrong, training wrong, and managing wrong — wrong for you and your practice and what you want.

We get lost, our vision and mission get lost, and our time and energy get sucked up in the hiring/training/ firing cycle. And we have a practice to nourish on top of the training. To teach and train and inspire with a mission and vision at the root of all of it is a lot when you are trying to build a practice, too.

So, very quickly you find yourself fed up with all of the training, and you decide, somewhat misguided, to just do it yourself. Then you end up trying to do the work of the whole team, and that's when resentment sets in.

Why can't I just get this right? Why can't I stop micromanaging? Why can't they get how important this is, and how insignificant that is? Do I need to spell out everything? Screw it! I will just do it myself.

This, my friend, is the trap. Hiring the wrong people for the wrong position, to end up putting even more work on your plate.

There was a time when I was new in practice, that I had the wrong combination of women working for me. None of them fit my practice. They did not see my vision for chiropractic and how it made the world different. Like, at all.

I hired each of them because that is what I was told I needed to do. I hired them because I liked them and I thought they were cool. I hired them because I thought I needed to have one person running this division, one person running that division, and I do what matters most for me to be doing — serve my people.

I got to a point where I hated going to work. I was working with a team of people who didn't want to be there, didn't get what I do, and frankly, didn't like me. I felt like at any given moment, I could feel their eyes roll so hard, that it would burn into my confidence, affecting the way that I served.

I was miserable.
I am not a manager.
In fact, I suck at it.

I can barely manage myself (at least at that time). I wanted to go to work to play in the greatness of all things healing and love and laughter, not to manage. I never had training in directing and managing. I was never taught accountability check-ins and team meeting structures.

So, I had to spend a ton of time and energy figuring it out. And it was a distraction from what I really wanted to do — serve great care.

My message got lost with other people working for me. I have a really clear vision of what I want to say, teach, and share with the community I serve.

People naturally make the assumption that whoever is sitting behind my desk, answering my phone, supporting my clients, gets that vision and represents it too.

I found it very difficult to fill part-time positions with people who shared the same vision, period. And the combination of skill, talent, and vision, wrapped up into a part-time position was a mere impossibility.

Over the years there were a few team members who fit the bill, but their talent was huge and my practice was just a temporary stepping stone for them.

Totally cool, but more work, more training, and more transition for me and my community.

So naturally, the solution for this very busy, multitasking, micromanaging, overwhelmed mama on a mission was to create new systems, systems that would not only work well for my practice, but give me dependency that was consistent! And that is exactly what I did.

2
PREPARING TO GO STAFFLESS

Most of us choose our craft from a strong desire to serve, a calling if you will. And then we go through training — the shape-shifting process of becoming a practitioner. By the time we complete our training, we are often left exhausted and depleted, feeling unprepared to serve.

I had nothing left after grad school. I was broke in every sense of the word. I had to start all over. I had to reconnect with my *why* that brought me to graduate school in the first place. I had to set my vision for practice straight, then create a plan for it.

I needed a real-deal action plan for what I wanted to do with this piece of paper that I had just spent ten years and over $100,000 earning.

My doctorate gave me the key to serving my community, but I had to build the path through which to do so.

I had been a professional student for a decade, and needed a transition plan to practice successfully and effectively. I didn't have one. At all. I scrambled, pounded pavement, and figured it out. But boy-oh-boy would it have been nice to have some direction.

I wanted to create a practice that was busy and successful and joyful. But I was totally burned out, unhealthy and stuck. Personally, I needed a reboot.

Many of my classmates that graduated with me were doing all kinds of cool stuff to prepare for starting practice: a month in the desert, traveling Europe for six months, a mentorship program with this guru and that guru.

Not me. I couldn't wait. I was hot to trot. I wanted nothing more than to get started, pull up my sleeves, find my people and serve them. Pronto. So, I did.

The truth is I had a ton of healing to. I was in no condition to lead and serve and teach and mentor. I was a hot mess and just getting hotter.

But my passion and commitment was stronger than the hot mess that was sending my life in a tizzy, and I pushed through.

I had a ton of growing up to do. And you know what, it all worked out. I was really young when I started practice, and I matured as my practice matured. I hit walls, fell down, and got back up. Each time I got back up, my ego deflated and my heart grew bigger. I was ready for more lessons and healing and serving. I was learning. I was growing up. I was figuring it all out, piece by piece, one struggle at a time.

That's why they call it *practice*, right? Practice, practice, practice — and eventually you figure it out.

I had to learn about overwhelm and making mistakes and figuring it out. We all get overwhelmed. We all get to a place where we feel like if one more thing happens, we will break.

So, where do we start? How do we shake the overwhelm?

Where to start?
Take a deep breath.
Put your feet on the floor.
Look down at your feet.
That, my friend, is your starting point.

Find your feet, and start there, right where you are with only what is in front of you. The rest has a way of working itself out.

Avoid burnout.

We are born with an internal clock - when to sleep, when to eat, when to cry, and on. As we mature, our clock matures. The demands we face naturally mature. Sometimes too much. Sometimes we push, too much, and the demands get overwhelming.

Sometimes we go past the line in the sand and stop listening. We go and go and go, until we can't go anymore. Then, we crash. And that is never good.

Yes, we have demands to meet. We have bills to pay. We have people to serve. We have a life that is waiting. We give and do and create and provide and boom — too much.

For me, burnout usually comes on slowly. I get physical and emotional signals. I do my best to ignore them as long as I can, because I really do like to keep going.

My signals: I start reacting to my kids in ways that I always have to go back and apologize for. I see the numbers on the scale creeping up and my clothes getting tighter on me. I feel sore in my body in places that I don't normally feel sore.

I stop connecting with the people who know me best because I'm afraid they're going to call me out on my lack of balance (side note, you need to have those people. If you don't…find them!).

The longer I'm in practice and the more stripes I earn, the quicker I am able to catch myself heading towards burnout. Sometimes the ability to slow down long enough to catch it and turn it around seems intangible.

But I am telling you now, develop this skill. Develop the skill of knowing your burnout signals and catching yourself before you hit the wall. Develop it now, and it will take you far.

It's one of the things I get asked about most. How do I refill, reboot, renew myself? So, I want to share a little of what's helped me. Here we go.

To keep my cool:
I work out every day. When I don't, I feel it.
I eat clean, real food.
I stay hydrated.
I spend time with people who get me.

I stay connected to my kids. I try to remember to get down and dirty and play with them, daily, I stay connected with my husband, who is my very best friend - always has been, always will be.

I rest. I nap. I play.
I buy things for myself that I really love. Not a lot of things, just things I really love.

I have to mention chiropractic here. I get adjusted, often (shout out to my guy, Dr. Wayne Rebarber). Chiropractic is key, and if you don't have a family chiropractor…just please. Go! Get one! Reach out to me if you need help finding them. I've got connections.

And I have hobbies. Some are silly, some not so much.

My favorite hobby — getting a new calendar. It may seem ridiculous to you, but nothing does it for me like walking down the calendar aisle at my local office supplies store and starting fresh with a brand new calendar.

It is a whole process. I have to touch every one, picture it in my life, in my bag, on my desk. Once I choose the right one, the ritual begins.

I go home, get my markers and highlighters out, and go for it. I reorganize my time, my appointments, my availability, my connection to my life. I do this at least a couple times a year.

Figure out your thing, your hobby, your list, your secret weapon. Everyone has them. We have to have them.

Back to burnout.
If I don't listen to the signs of burnout, and sometimes I don't, I usually get to a point of pain. Sometimes I hurt so bad that I can't even move. It stops me. Then a break is forced. There is nothing worse than a forced life break, not able to do this and that with my family and friends — it is never fun.

There are days, sometimes weeks, when I just don't feel like it. Believe me, during these times…I want to hang like a beached whale on a warm, sunny day. These are the days that I don't feel like listening and doing my part. I feel like laying on the couch and eating bon-bons. I'm too sore, too run down, too needy, too all of it. Sometimes I choose to use the couch like a life preserver. Sometimes I need it. I need to rest, to regroup. But I can very easily stay there for too long. I am getting better and better at catching this. Getting back to self-care.

The rest is needed. The rest is how I avoid burnout.

If I don't take the rest, I *do* burnout. There are signs, little at first then big. And if I don't listen, they only get bigger. They take over. Pain, fatigue, annoyance — my inner bitch comes out and it is never good.

Find your thing. Find what does it for you. Discover how you like to reconnect and renew. Get really familiar with your signs, your signals of burnout. Avoid it at all costs.

Listen for the signals, or they will get louder and louder, and eventually take over. After many years in practice and 100,000+ adjustments served, I am here to tell you that listening to your signs is imperative.

Be sure, more than sure, to have systems in place to check in with yourself — checkpoints, if you will.

Look for the signals of burnout — identify it when it is happening, and nip it right in the bud!

One of the first things we do with our new students in SEWP School (details coming) is pair you up with an accountability buddy. Someone to call you on your shit, hold you accountable, and celebrate your growth.

Find a buddy y'all! They can make or break your practice experience. Have regular calls with them. Let them in, let them get to know you!

Daily and weekly checkpoints keep me on track. I know what I need to do each day and each week to stay energized and centered. You have to create your own. The balance equation is different for everyone.

I'm gonna provide an easy self care list, create your own. Use it, regularly.

The easy self-care list.

Daily:
- For every hour you sit in front of the computer, move your body for ten minutes (to the point of sweat). So, for 4 hours on the computer, 40 minutes of sweat.
- Drink plenty of water - stay hydrated.
- Have days off - at least one per week. You need time to just be.
- Meal prep - don't neglect your nutrition. It needs to be at the top of the list every day.
- Turn the screens off at a certain time of the day, and don't turn them back on until the next day. For me - 8PM to 8AM. Off.

Weekly:
- Start the week with a master to-do list.
- Regularly recommit to your ideal schedule (coming up).

- Have a family meeting at the end of each week to review wins, challenges, and responsibilities for the upcoming week.
- Follow your task list for your practice marketing plan. Do a little each week to avoid all-at-once overwhelm.

Success starts with a vision.

There are some very specific moments throughout our lives that we stay completely connected to, unseparated by time. I have a handful of them. One in particular inspired many aspects of my practice career.

Flashback 22 years ago. I was a bright-eyed, recent grad at a chiropractic seminar. I was chatting with a very gentle man who had been in practice since I was born. At that time, he was coming up on his 30th year anniversary.

He was kind and solid, he had a wrinkly, lovable face and huge, warm hands (most old-timer chiropractors have huge, warm hands).

He gently asked me what my vision for my practice looked like.

Hunh? My vision? Please repeat.

Well, my vision is to get out of debt and pay off my student loans. My vision is to lose the 40 pounds I put on during graduate school. My vision is to quit smoking so that I can feel authentic in my expression in the world. Is that what you mean?

He took his huge hands, and lovingly placed them on my shoulders. He leaned in and whispered words that have carried me for over 20 years. He simply said, "success needs to start with a vision, then it can become a reality."

Ok…that is some deep shit right there, I thought. But *hunh*?

I totally understand what he was saying now, but as a new doctor he left me clueless — scratching my head and feeling once again that there was some book somewhere that I missed, that everyone else read, that taught the rules of how things were.

Not to mention, I would have done anything to have him walk around with those big hands on my shoulders at all times, to guide me where to go right and where to go left. I had no direction, no vision.

I took some time, some paper and a few great pens, and got to work. I asked myself the right questions, and my vision came to life in a matter of hours.

I wrote out what I wanted, who I wanted to serve, why I wanted to serve them, where I wanted to serve, and how I wanted to serve. It was all in there. Maybe I just needed the right questions. Maybe that's all we ever need.

Fast forward 20 years later. My vision is crystal clear to me. I have specific statements that connect me to my vision, that I carry around in my back pocket (in my phone really), at all times.

I know what I want to create for myself this month, this quarter, and this year. I know where I want to be 10 years from now. I know that to get there, I'm going to need to have a plan, and my plan is in place. I also know that with each moment, that plan can change. And I am good with that.

But I didn't get there overnight, and I wasn't really ready for the question when it hit me. I was baffled.

So here I am, asking you the question. You ready?

…..

…..

…..

Hey friend, what is your vision for success?

Create your vision statement.

It's time to define success in your own words, so that when you reach it, you know it. Once you have realized your vision of success, you may find that it's a lot closer to fruition than you thought!

PEN TO PAPER
create a vision

What do you want to create for your practice in the next few months?

The next year?

The next five years?

What do you want to create for your home-life in the next few months?

The next year?

The next five years?

What do you want to create for your health in the next few months?

The next year?

The next five years?

Narrow your answers down to three very specific, concise statements.

...

There you have it my friend. Feel free to jump in our community group (see end of book for access) and share your vision with us! We are waiting to hear it!

Your building blocks - core values.

Whether we realize it or not, at the root of each decision we make, we can find a core value driving that decision. Our values mold us, shift us, direct us, and run our lives. They are the blocks that we build healthy foundations with. One at a time, value by value.

A clear connection with each of our core values can very possibly be a significant missing piece for the staffless practitioner.

On the other hand, not being connected to your values (what they are and how powerful they are) can be a huge roadblock to success.

If you are running a practice without staff, you are going to have to keep a lot of balls up in the air at all times. If your core values keep you connected to why you want to run a staffless practice in the first place, your commitment to sticking to your systems and procedures is likely to strengthen.

This commitment will keep you driven to moving in the right direction. I promise.

Listen up people — there is nothing worse than bad care, especially if you spend a decent amount of time trying to get the practice thing right.

Ugh, bad care — the kind of care that leaves you shaking your head and wondering how the practice is staying open. The kind of care that makes you wonder how they don't know how much better it could be. How fun practice can be. How much life and light and love there is to let it. Ok, so I go overboard. But you get the point.

The cold, hard chair wait.

Since as far back as I can remember, I have hated going to the doctor's office. The cold, hard chairs, shiny floor, the irrelevant pictures on the walls.

The ladies behind the glass window who look at you like you are bothering them by just breathing. And the smell. Oh man, the smell. Like every toxic cleaner out there was poured into a bucket and smeared aimlessly all over the floor with a moldy, dirty rag. Yep, you know the smell.

Sometimes I have to go. I have to do my grown-up visits at my grown-up doctor's appointments.

Here's the way this usually goes down:

I walk in. I'm hit with the smell. The lights are so bright and noisy, already my eyes hurt.

There are three other women in the waiting room. They look annoyed, like they have been there for a while. How long? Is their appointment time before mine?

Am I going to be that annoyed in 30 minutes when I am still sitting there?

I walk up to the counter, to NOT be greeted by a grumpy lady sitting behind a desk that has very clearly never been fitted for her.

It is too high and she is too little and the chair is too big. But what do I know? I'm just a chiropractor.

She looks up at me, slides open the wall of glass separating us, takes a sip of her diet soda (it's 10 a.m.) and says, *"Insurance card and license, please?"* in the most annoyed voice possible. Like I am wrong for being there, like there is no wait and I am not paying and she is not loving me in this moment.

Did I do something wrong? Maybe I have B.O.? No *hello* or *good morning* or *sorry for the wait*?

Yep. I am a wise ass. So, my response goes something like, "Oh good morning, and how are you?" usually provoking a smile which cracks the code for some human banter and connection.

The truth is, I am probably the first person who has asked her how she is doing all morning. The truth is, she is probably a lovely person, and totally overworked, underpaid and not appreciated. Probably.

Then the wait. The awkward sit on the cold, hard chair with the water-stained magazines that are six months old and the sounds of the door opening and closing only to watch three, four, five more clients go through the same rotation to the cold, hard chair.

They join me in the awkward silence. Everything in me wants to start chatting, bring joy to the room, pop the huge bubble of silence.

Maybe I should start singing a show tune, like on the top of my lungs? This could be a chance to lift their day, share some joy, crack some people up? Maybe I could even tell them about chiropractic?

But I don't. I sit. I wait. I think about all the funny things I could be saying in this very awkward moment.

When I finally get called in to see the doctor, I am greeted with another twenty-minute wait. Only for this wait, I'm in a gown, half naked, the room I'm in is smaller than my closet, and the door is closed. Did I mention I don't like small spaces? My ass is stuck to the paper that covers the cold exam table. I feel like a lab rat. And, if possible, it smells even worse in here.

Finally, the doctor comes in for three minutes, meets with me, leaves, and $300 later I get on the schedule to do it all again in a year.

Don't they know I have shit to do? Don't they know I have a name and a schedule and feelings? Don't they know how wrong all of this is? Do they value my time, my name, my story?

Don't they care that the office smells and the lights hurt and the chairs suck? Don't they value what is good, and right, and true? And if not, what do they value, and how does that align with my wanting to be here?

They don't. Because this is the system.

This is what has become the norm, the acceptable. No connection to core values. Only connection to the system. The bottom line, the dollars and cents of it all.

But it can change. It *has to* change. It can change for each office, each practitioner, each client.

All of the points that pain me about the typical doctor's visit have become my focal points for creating not only clinical greatness, but also academic greatness for my students.

My ways are unique. They are against the grain, out of the box, and all with intention. My office truly is an expression of my core values, and my clients feel it from the first time they experience it. They love the warmth, the attention to detail, all of the senses being celebrated in unique ways.

I created for my clients, exactly what I would love to experience as a client. You can too.

Discover your core values.

Ok, let's do it. Let's discover your core values. When you break down all of your actions, decisions, the near-and-dear-to-your-heart components of your life — at the root will always be your core values. The discovery of core values is SO IMPORTANT that it is one of the first things we have our new SEWP Students do.

As long as I have a close connection to my core values, I can make decisions with a clear head and an even clearer heart. If I disregard my core values when making decisions, I regret it every time. I literally keep a printout of them on my desk. I want to stay connected to them. Especially where I work. I like to take a peek at them when making big business decisions or if I am feeling scattered.

My values are there to hold all of my decisions up to, like a mirror. The decisions either fit my values, or they don't. If they do, I lean in. If they don't — next.

Take some time to discover if your personal core values and your practice core values differ. Sometimes they do. More often they don't.

For example, you may have a very strong connection to the core value of *excitement* in your personal life; however, you may feel strongly about avoiding the experience of *excitement* for your practice — it may feel like too much. Does that make sense? I sure hope so, friend.

Your turn to find your values.

Here you go — a list of core values, examples that could very possiblly JUMP off the page, smack you in the face, and provide instant direction for you! Circle the ones that do *that.* Remember, there are so many more, this is just a starting list. Pick five, or six, maybe even seven. Sit with them for a day or two. Write them on a post-it, study them. Can you narrow them down? Can you combine a couple of them?

Compassion
Freedom
Organization
Joy
Abundance
Authenticity
Honesty
Excitement
Creativity
Release
Centeredness
Health
Independence
Strength

Security
Respect
Optimism
Positivity
Humor
Efficiency
Connection
Collaboration
Ease
Humility

….

Once you have picked your words, play with them. Yep, a game. Ready?

In walks *the why game*.

You know the one. The game that most eight-year-olds will play until they are blue in the face, asking *why* to anything you throw at them until there is no more.

The why game goes something like this:
I work out every day.
Why?
Because it makes me feel really good.
Why?
Because it clears my head.
Why?
Because I sweat and let go of whatever I need to.
Why?

Because I need inner peace, a fresh start each day, a new beginning to greet my next day.
Why?
Because.

No more answers.

At the root...*inner peace. Fresh start.*
At the root...*peace & clarity.*

Boom...there they are.

Build your mission statement.

Ok, you've got the core values piece. Now you are going to take them, marry them together, and build your mission statement. As you watch your mission statement come to life know that you are creating such a HUGE foundational piece to a successful staffless practice. Your mission statement will provide a platform from which all big practice decisions are made.

You want your mission statement to tell your community who you are, what is important to you, how you serve, what you do, and perhaps what you do not do. Share it! Post it! Put it on your site. Let the world see your mission statement and know it is yours!

Allow your mission statement to also keep you anchored to your core values. Keep it printed out in multiple places throughout your office. Stay connected to it.

Think about the hard to deal with moments of practice and life, and how powerful it could be to have a mission statement anchoring you, each step of the way.

…

Let's use my core values, for an example, string them together, and bring my mission statement to fruition. Ready? Here we go.

Core Values:
Integrity
Abundance
Joy
Excitement
Wellness
Organization

Mission Statement:
We create *joy*-filled health solutions for our clients, with *integrity* at the forefront of each exchange. Our well-*organized* client communication systems accomplish *abundant* milestones; offering *exciting*

wellness discovery for our participants.

3
AUTOMATE YOUR COMMUNICATIONS

It is really important to me that my clients know that my office is ready for them, my practice is organized, and I have prepared for them with a ton of thought.

The phone, the schedule, the appointments, the receipts, the admin tasks — it all needs a solution. Without staff. Without me. Automated. Running on its own. When I made the decision to go staffless, I needed to create each puzzle piece for effective, automated client communications and set them in the right spot.

Eventually the communication puzzle came together, piece by piece, to create the most beautiful, self-run, family practice systems. Years later these systems are still rocking my very busy, joy-filled practice.

I've been a chiropractor for a long time, and I have served all types of people. I am also a self-proclaimed geek when it comes to automating my client communication. Nothing floats my boat more than to hear cheers from my clients about how my automation rocks their world, too.

I am 150% a free spirit. I take care of some high executive, fancy-pants VIP's. Even though we are worlds apart, and I'm dancing around my office with my barefoot groove and my essential oils, and they are coming in with their thousand-dollar suits and their Louis Vuitton bags, they get that I honor their time. They get my business sense, and how much attention I have put into avoiding unnecessary headaches and giving bad care.

They get how easy it is to be a client in my world, how supportive my systems are, and how sensitive I am to never wasting their time. Totally cool.

I knew that most of what my staff was doing could be done in a quarter of the time if it was automated, like the five minutes it took to make an appointment for Sally (listening to this story and that detail on the phone) could be accomplished in 30 seconds.

The super-bill that took ten minutes to type up and get in the mail, could be sent in 10 seconds if set up right.

I figured out how to automate every nook and cranny of my office. Every client communication and transaction (where applicable).

And listen, these solutions work. Really well.

It has always been huge to me to not let my personal style or my message drop through automation. I wanted each of my client systems to still feel like me and my style. Not so easy to do, but for sure once it was set, it was set. I'm going to show you how.

Let's dive into the automation discovery work for your practice. If you have staff, have them read through these systems. It could really shift their experience as a team member in your office.

Read through with an open mind, think outside the box of ordinary and things that should and could and would.

Remember, your practice is a reflection of your unique mark in the world. Don't take shortcuts when planning this out, think of the *who, what, where, when, and why* you want to create for your practice experience and make it great.

Let the phone ring.

It's 10 a.m. on a Monday morning. My office is hoppin'. My practice members want to get in and out quickly, to move on to the ten other things they have on their list for this morning. They are hungry for some great chiropractic care to get their week started off on the right foot.

Speaking of hungry, because I got up late this morning, my kid missed the bus, my shower was cold, the dog left me a treat in my favorite shoes, I couldn't find my keys — like it was really one of those mornings. And yes, I was the last on the list — so no breakfast. I'm hungry, but it's going to have to wait — along with the messages, the mail, the bathroom stop, and most of all, Sally.

Sally is standing at my desk wondering why three people went into my treatment room before her. Like, I can hear her thinking that. Like, she is the most important person on my schedule, even though she walked in five minutes late and owes me for the last three visits.

She is the one — she's the *Sally* I let push my buttons and get away with the late thing and the look thing and the guilt thing.

We all have a Sally, right?

Did I mention the phone is ringing? But, guess what Buttercup!? It's all good because that is one box I have checked off. That is one compartment of my very complicated morning that I don't have to remember, think about, or manage — my phone system.

I know the phone is ringing. I hear it. One gentle ring just to tell me it's happening — I like to know what balls are in the air when it comes to my practice pieces, and I want to know that the phone ball is in the air, without having to catch it. So, I created all the systems to set me up for that moment.

Sally, bring it on.

Whoever is calling my office right now is going to land at a message that will give them exactly what they are looking for.

If it is a new person calling, they will be properly directed. If it is a current client calling, they too will get what they are looking for.

And if it is a spam call, they will hang up without wasting my time, and go back to where they came from because that is exactly how I set my phone system up — so that me, and Sally, and the other clients waiting for my service, and my rumbling tummy, get exactly what we need in the moment. All of the balls are in the air, and I've got this.

The Do-it-all-er.

From an early age Jess learned that if something was going to be completed right, she was going to need to do it herself. When she was twelve her mom signed her up for ballet classes, signing all the right forms, getting the best shoes and the cutest outfit. The schedule was on the fridge. She was set. Then the day came for class. Nobody was there to take her. The schedule got dropped. Jess was home alone, with her sparkly ballet bag and her new shoes, disappointed.

Her whole life, she never seemed to be able to lean on others to get to where she wanted to be. So, she learned that in order to accomplish the things that she wanted to accomplish, she was going to have to do them herself. She became a *do-it-all-er*.

When it came to practice, Jess got really good at doing everything for everyone. She never wanted staff. Depending on others didn't work for her. Her need to get it all done worked, until it didn't.

A few years into practice, Jess was facing burnout. There were people pulling her in every direction. Even with the greatest strength and the best tools, nobody could do all the things that she signed up to do. She didn't know how to say NO when she needed to, so she said YES way too much.

Seeing things in retrospect always brings clarity. Looking back, Jess can see that she was spending a lot of time each week doing things for her clients that they really could have done for themselves.

Her issue was that she didn't trust that if they said they were going to get them done, they were actually going to get them done. So, she didn't feel safe enough to put the success of these practice systems into the clients' hands.

She had to learn to let go. She had to learn to give some of it to her clients. She had to trust that if they wanted her care they would sign the things and schedule the spots and show up at the right times.

The truth is (in my experience) that people *want* to participate in their care. They want to be responsible for their part. Doing it all for them takes away a very important piece of the client's experience.

Jess needed to create one-and-done systems to make it easy for them to do their part. Once she did just that, she lifted such a weight from her shoulders. She could finally enjoy practice again, free up her schedule, and give her clients the opportunity to participate more in their own care.

Use your phone as a client directory.

Let's go on a journey with your office phone. Let's turn it into an automated manager directing people to the solutions they are calling for without you needing to be in the mix, even more important, without losing the personal touch your clients have come to expect.

Freedom through automation awaits you if you create your phone systems just right! Remember to keep it simple. Simplicity truly is the name of the game when it comes to your office phone!

You can program your phone to direct people to self book, answer questions about you and your practice leave new and existing clients greetings, direction, and assurance, and much, much more. Set your phone up to work for you so that when you are in the office, all you need to do is what you are best at, what you are paid the big bucks for, the stuff that totally floats your boat!

Let the phone do the rest. All the scheduling, directing, question answering, Sally redirecting, and more is waiting for you.

Phone basics, 101.

Please remember, these suggestions are what I have found work for me and my practice. You do you. Super, super important!

When to answer the phone.
It is really important that you figure out how much you want to personally connect with each call coming in. How much of the process do you want to participate with?

Use your discretion for when and where you make yourself available. Some practitioners will answer the phone when they are at the desk doing busywork.

Others will create a recording that provides solutions for all of the reasons someone could be calling. Remember, if automation is the key for your practice success, starting with the phone is a no-brainer.

What to say when you do answer the phone.
If you do grab the phone, keep it short and sweet. Just the name of your practice with voice inflection (your voice goes up). And smile. Always smile. Smiling really does make a difference — it is really hard to sound grumpy or tired when you are smiling. And grumpy is no good when it comes to answering the phone. You want to be light and sweet and kind. You never know what situation is on the other end of the phone.

Saying much more than your practice name when answering the phone can feel like too much to the caller. I have been on the other end of *Thank you for calling...Family Practice, my name is ...I am thrilled to help you make it an awesome day, what can I do for you?* No way! What if it's not an awesome day? Do I really want to be thanked? Do I really need to know who I am speaking to? If so, add it. If not, drop it. My suggestion is to keep it short and sweet.

Don't tell them it's you!

Let that unfold naturally unless they ask who they're speaking with. Often, if they know they are speaking to the practitioner, they will assume it is a good time to tell you all about it. But you want *that* conversation to happen at the right time, when you are in the right headspace for it. You want to catch that ball when you are in the catcher's position, when you have the right pen and the right paper in front of you, ready to listen, study, and serve.

Personally, my people all know me, and they know if I answer the phone, I am going to want to chitchat with them. So, if I want to chat it up, I answer. Otherwise, my voicemail gives them what they are calling for.

When you can't or don't want to answer the phone.

Create your solutions to get your people what they need without having to be in the mix! Let callers go to a directive (tells them where to go), content-rich (lots of information), precise (gets right to the point) voicemail.

Rest assured when you are busy running the show, your callers who go to voicemail are landing in a well-designed, directive funnel.

How to get people familiar with your system.
If you follow our system, from your first conversation (usually text or email), your clients will know that automation is key for your practice success and the success of their administrative care.

I share my practice communication system with my clients repeatedly (visit one, two, and three — more coming). They know if they want to get in touch with me, texting is their best bet. For my practice, texting is the name of the game. I use my templates (pre-written texts) to get my people what they are looking for, quickly.

My texting number is offered everywhere someone could be looking to connect with me; on my voicemail, in my email signature, and on my website. So just to reiterate, if by chance my clients do call the office, the message they end up listening to provides just about any solution they could be calling for.

Some will call. Some forget my system (as most of them are moving through the world faster than the speed of light and don't commit my practice systems to memory). I have them covered, as they land in my message funnel.

Answering Service? Virtual Assistant?
You have to figure out what works for you and your practice. If and when you need to delegate phone management out to a Virtual Assistant (VA) or an answering service, you can provide them with the scripts to manage your phone systems correctly.

If you feel really strongly about people calling your office and getting a live person, an answering service could really work for your practice.

I've never loved the idea of having a VA or assistant answer my calls coming in. I want to touch them. I want each call to have my message, my purpose, and my love. I for sure need control on this one, and have not been able to master the balance of delegating the calls and feeling connected to them.

The system I use instead, really works. It is not only fluid and complete, but it is automated too. More coming.

Avoid the chitchat!
There is one in every bunch! A Sally who wants to tell you about the kids, the grandkids, the shoes, the

house, the cat, the *whatever you will listen to*. Again, if this is your jam, listen up! But for most of us, our time is so pressed that we really need to avoid phone chitchat.

There are ways to gracefully end conversations. You can say something like, *Oh wait, what time is it? I have a call I have to be on*, or *I'd love to hear what you have to say, but I am really tight on time today*.

Ask them to hold the phone for a second, put it on mute, come back 10 seconds later, let them know you have to go.

Say what you mean, mean what you say, don't say it meanly.

For me, I'm too busy and do too much! I rarely have time in the office for chitchatting with my clients on the phone. I just can't. Every once in a while, I'll get stuck or caught off guard with a story that seems to have a VERY long beginning, and no end in sight.

Don't get me wrong, I love to hear how my people are doing and what is going on in their lives, but I'm also pressed for time, and sometimes being pressed too hard is too much.

And…sometimes the chitchat feels really necessary to your clients, so be sensitive to the situation. Have a quick resource for your people to book time with you if they need to talk more in a private consult. I have to use my discretion. You do too. This is the shit we learn in the school of hard knocks. Experience. And it matters, a lot.

For some of my people, I am the only person they want to confide in, and chatting with me is really imperative to our relationship. So, I may just schedule them solo for a few visits until I feel that they don't need the one-on-one so much. There is a fine line between never listening, and being a doormat for aimless stories. Find the line, and stick to it. There is nothing worse than a practitioner who doesn't listen. Well…almost *nothing*.

Dodge the spam calls!
Most phones these days show the number the call is coming in from. If you don't recognize the number, let it go to your voicemail. If it is a spam call, you most likely won't get a voicemail.

If they are NOT a spam caller, they will be heading into a directive voicemail to get them what they need.

There are sites that you can register on for do-not-call lists. I have done this in the past, and it seems to help for a short time (six months or so), then I have to register again.

Cell? Landline? Online phone system?

Ok, let's break it down — no need for overwhelm here. Remember, keeping it simple is the name of the game!

<u>Cell phone</u>: 100% personal preference. If you use your cell for the practice, you need to have boundaries with it. It's REALLY easy to get into that rut, and one day you wake up to realize that you have become THAT PERSON who is always on their phone. Don't do that. Your life deserves more.

We want to avoid burnout at all costs, and the cell phone can certainly take you down the road to burnout. But *it is* convenient. There are so many fancy functions you can do with your cell that you can't necessarily do with a landline. Just be clean and clear with your time and attention to it.

<u>Landline</u>: I use a landline for my practice. I always have. We've had the same phone number for over 20 years and I love that. I have looked into complicated systems and have used some over the years, but I always resort back to a simple landline.

I have one solid base to my phone system at my desk (we literally don't have a front desk in my office, just a standing desk for the phone and my stuff). Because it is attached to the wall, it is never misplaced. It has extensions (portable phones) throughout the office, in case I need to grab the phone in a pinch. It is rare that

I do, but this girl can never be too prepared.

My only concern for anyone just starting out is that a landline may be a thing of the past soon. Use your discretion here. Ask around in your circles, and use the system that resonates best with you and your practice.

There are some sophisticated online phone systems worth investigating. Just keep in mind cost, adaptability, and benefit of the service you are considering.

Create boundaries around the phone!
For me and my family, on Friday night the phone goes off for the weekend, and I pick it up on Sunday night to prep for the week. You may feel that you don't want to miss an important call from an important person. Here's the deal — they will call back, or better yet, they will follow your system and leave you their information where it needs to be left!

My cell number is not used for my practice unless I have a mama in labor or a dear friend in need. Even then, I tend to be choosy with my time. My kids will only be kids once — I don't want to miss it.

Wearing a smart watch, smart?
Wearing a smart watch has benefits, but it also means that you are always on when wearing it. Of course, there are settings you can play with to turn alerts on

and off. However, when you're doing a million things during client hours, having a connection on your wrist is a quick, easy way to stay connected. You can still see the office texts coming in for same-day requests and any pertinent fires that need to be addressed while you are with clients.

I wear a smart watch while I am serving in the office, I like the flexibility it provides. I have a tendency to be a bit spacey when I am adjusting, and I never remember where I put my cell.

So, having a connection to it on my wrist gives me some sort of false sense of security that I have become used to. I like to be connected to my kids, and my watch buzzes every time they text me. If I start to feel distracted by the watch, I just take it off.

Easy, peezy.

I talk about texting a lot. It is just easy and quick and convenient. Much more to come, but here is some to get started with.

Texting is the way.
Texting is a quick form of communication to get Sally on your schedule for Thursday at 5. She texts you a request, you text back a template that you have already created to reply with a yes, a no, or perhaps suggest a different time. You click a button in response to her request, and it is done.

You will have a dependable method to address what needs to get addressed. Most of your texting will be automated responses that you create once and BOOM — you're set. Gone are the days of unplanned typos, fat thumbs messing up messages, or reactive, in the moment, inappropriate comments that you wish you could un- text.

More on texting coming, hang tight.

The voicemail message funnel system.

Yep, funnel. Think of a funnel for sand. Starting with large opening up top, we pour the sand through to set it in motion. Then we can divide it up to go in different directions with fun tubes and wheels and filters, and rejoin all of the sand at the bottom of the funnel.

We can do the same thing with calls coming into your practice. They all come in, they all get directed, they all end up in the same spot, getting your callers' needs met. Nothing beats a good phone message to get the right words to the right people at the right time. We are going to create the perfect funnels for your callers to get to the solutions they are calling for. Even more important, all of this will be automated, taking you and your time out of the mix. You will get the hang of this, I promise.

I have such a clear memory of recording my DURING HOURS funnel in front of one of my practice members, she happened to walk in while I was doing it. She listened. She was dazzled by the fact that I had memorized the entire thing and how much sense it made. She loved it's clarity and direction.

Little did she know how used to recording it I got, how instrumental and unforgettable each piece was, or how quickly I commit things to memory. But her dazzlement struck me, and stuck with me, and told me that there was something special to it. Something I would need to do with it. And here I am, sharing it with you.

Create your voicemail message funnels.

There are two ways of doing this — you can be the practitioner that updates their voicemail message a couple times a day with hours and information relevant to that day, changing the voicemail when the day is over to your after-hours voicemail; or you can have a one-and-done voicemail, which is less relevant to the time and day your callers are reaching out, and evergreen (always relevant to the time the person is calling in). Remember, evergreen is good.

Evergreen = automated....most of the time.

I have done the daily updating thing and I found it got old, fast. I now keep my one-and-done voicemail on my system at all times. I only change it if something unique is happening (like an office closing or holiday hours).

Whichever you choose, I strongly suggest having these voicemail message scripts ready:

- A script for DURING CLIENT HOURS - for when you are in
- A script for AFTER CLIENT HOURS - for when your office is closed
- A ONE AND DONE script - does not address whether or not you are in - *evergreen*

The nine pillars of a voicemail message funnel.

Your funnels need solid pillars, as they are going to be holding up the foundation of your entire practice communication system.

Here are nine pillars to all effective voicemail message funnels:

1. **Your practice name and location** - sound happy when you say it, like there is a party coming out of your mouth. It will take you a long way!

2. **Your name and title** - speak clearly, and again, sound happy.

3. **A warm greeting** - something sweet to show your personality.

4. **What information the message will provide and how to bypass it** - give a quick outline of what your message funnel will provide. Keep it short. Something like *this message will give you directions to get the help that you need in the most effective way, including our current office hours, our website, and our best form of immediate communication*.

Ask your phone company how your callers can bypass the rest of the message and share it with them.

5. **Address each type of caller** (new clients, current clients, clients coming back) - think back to the last ten calls you answered in the office. You could probably categorize your callers in one of three groups: new clients looking to get started with you, current clients looking for an admin solution, or clients who have not been around for a while looking to come back. It may be worth your time to do a study of your incoming calls for a few days to ensure this is true for your practice.

Address what <u>current clients</u> should do - usually my current clients are calling to hear my hours or get a quick answer (like my website or my availability that day).

Address what <u>people coming back</u> should do - most people coming back to my office after a long leave need to start with a private consult and an exam (re-evaluation). That needs to be set up through my website, so I send them there.

Address what <u>new people</u> should do - I send new people to my website. There is a warm video waiting there for them, and very clear directions on how to book their initial consultation with me.

6. **Your website** - repeat it twice, speak slowly. It may be the first time they are hearing your site address and they may be doing ten other things while they are calling you, so be sure to repeat yourself!

Side note: my website is super clear and easy to navigate so that people know which button to click to get to where they want to go. Don't make your site complicated.

7. **Your hours** - for all the message funnels, you want to list your regular hours. For same-day and after-hours message funnels, provide the relevant information (hours you are in, when you will be back, etc.)

8. **The best way to get the information they need** - I always suggest leading your callers to texting you for admin needs, go to your site for appointment booking, or leave a message if they are calling for a more detail-driven need.

9. **A warm exit -** Keep it short and sweet. *Make today awesome*, or *have a great day*, or *take great care of your health today*.

Tips for funnel success:
- Most phones have a way to make the recording on your system repeat itself instead of giving your callers the options of leaving a message. You may want to go this route if you don't want to deal with messages.
- Find out if your callers can press a button (in my area it's the # key) to skip the voicemail. If they can, state it in the beginning.

- Remember, first state what the recording will include.
- Many voicemail programs offer a feature to email you a transcript of each message left. This could be a really useful tool, something you could perhaps have sent to a VA.
- Don't forget to smile when recording your office message. It really does make a difference.
- Have a happy, warm tone to your voice. Think of how you would want to be greeted, what kind of message you would want to hear if you were calling your office.
- When you're saying phone numbers or a website address, speak slowly, and repeat yourself.
- Remember, this can all be changed and updated as your practice evolves.

DURING CLIENT HOURS funnel.

This is the message clients will hear if they call your office during client hours. Think nine pillars and give them the information they need, relevant details regarding same-day requests, etc.

Start with your rules.
You need to have rules (guides) for your office when it comes to your hours and availability.

First decide if you want to offer your clients same day requested appointments. What office policy do you want to implement regarding seeing people an hour after they request you? Is it too much for you? Do you enjoy the spontaneity of same-day appointments or do you need more consistency?

Once you have gotten clear on this, get to work with your during client hours script.

Here is the DURING CLIENT HOURS script I use for my office:

You have reached LightSource Chiropractic, located at ADDRESS. This is Dr. Jodi, your family chiropractor and I am so glad you called. Today is Monday, April 15th and I am in the office until 6.

This message will leave you information about our practice and how to get to us ASAP. To bypass it, press the # key now and leave us a message.

If you are a new client, welcome to our practice, Feel free to learn more about us online at WEBSITE for all of your admin and scheduling needs.

If you are a long-lost client coming back, welcome home! Please go to our website to book a re-evaluation.

If you are a current client looking for an appointment for today or later this week, leave the time you are looking for at the beep. Or better yet, text me! We have walk-in times available at 3, 4:15 and 5:50.

You can find most of your admin answers on our website at WEBSITE. That's WEBSITE.

I am serving the best in chiropractic on Monday, Thursday, and Friday from 10-12 and 4-6.

Texting us is the best way to get to us ASAP. You can text NUMBER. Again the number to text is NUMBER. Thank you for calling and make today awesome.

...

You see that? Everyone who could possibly be calling for my service is addressed. I am providing relevant, pertinent information to get them the solutions they are seeking. I am directing them through the funnel, to get to the next step of their process.

Build your practice DURING CLIENT HOURS script.

It will be comprised of the original nine pillars plus the two in bold:

- Your practice name and location
- Your name and title
- **Today's date and what time you are in until**
- A warm greeting

- What information this message will provide and how to bypass it
- Address each type of caller (new clients, current clients, clients coming back)
- Your website
- Your regular hours
- **Today's available walk-in hours**
- The best way to get the information they need
- A warm exit

Side note: Leave your available walk-in times for today and how they can grab one if this floats your boat. It sinks mine, so I don't do it.

PEN TO PAPER
during client hours

Practice name and location:

Your name and title:

Today's date and what time you are in until:

A warm greeting:

What this message will provide and how to bypass it:

Address what new people should do:

Address what current clients should do:

Address what people coming back should do:

Your website (if not mentioned already):

Your regular hours:

Leave your available walk-in times for today and how they can grab one:

Your best form of communication:

A warm exit:

AFTER HOURS CLIENT funnel.

This is the message people will hear if they call your office <u>after hours</u>. It is going to be really similar to what you just did for during client hours script with a few tweaks. Remember, think nine pillars — give them the information they need and relevant details regarding any requests they may have.

Your **AFTER HOURS CLIENT** funnel will include the following:
- Your practice name and location
- Your name and title
- A warm greeting
- **A reminder that the office is currently closed, and when you will be in next**
- What information this message will provide and how to bypass it
- Address each type of caller (new clients, current clients, clients coming back)
- Your website
- Your regular hours
- The best way to get the information they need
- A warm exit

Here is the AFTER CLIENT HOURS script I use for my office:

You have reached LightSource Chiropractic, located at ADDRESS HERE.

This is Dr. Jodi, your Family Chiropractor and I am so glad you called. Our office is currently closed, but we will reopen on Thursday at 10AM.

This message will leave you information about our practice and how to get to us ASAP. To bypass it, press the # key now and leave us a message.

If you are a new client, welcome to our practice, you can find us online at WEBSITE to find all of your admin and scheduling needs.

If you are a long-lost client coming back, welcome home! Please go to our website to book a re-evaluation.

For my current clients looking for a spot this week, just shoot me a text of what time works for you.

You can find most of your admin answers on our website at WEBSITE.

I am serving the best in chiropractic on Monday, Thursday and Friday from 10-12 and 4-6. Texting us is the best way to get to us ASAP. You can text PHONE NUMBER. Again that's PHONE NUMBER.

Thank you for calling and make today awesome.

PEN TO PAPER
after client hours

Your practice name and location:

Your name and title:

A warm greeting:

A reminder that the office is currently closed, and when you will be in next:

What information this message will provide and how to bypass it:

Address each type of caller (new clients, current clients, clients coming back):

Your website:

Your regular hours:

The best way to get the information they need:

A warm exit:

Good. Done. Next....

ONE AND DONE funnel.

This is it! I love this solution for my practice, and I rarely change it. This message addresses all requests coming in, regardless of whether your caller is calling while you are in the office or sitting on the baseball field with your kid.

Once again, think nine pillars — give them the information they need, and relevant details regarding any requests they may have.

Here is my ONE AND DONE script:
You have reached LightSource Chiropractic, located at ADDRESS HERE. This is Dr. Jodi, your Family Chiropractor and I am so glad you called.

We are in the office on Tuesdays and Thursdays from 10-12 and 4-6 and Saturdays from 10-12.

You can find most of your admin answers on our website at WEBSITE HERE. That's WEBSITE.

This message is going to give you all of the directions you need to get what you want. To bypass it, press the # key now and leave us a message. It may take some time to get back to you, but we will.

Texting us is the best way to get to us ASAP. You can text NUMBER HERE. Again that's NUMBER HERE.

If you are a new client, welcome to our practice, go to WEBSITE HERE for all of your admin and scheduling needs.

If you are a long-lost client coming back, welcome home! Please go to our website to book a re-evaluation.

If you are a current client looking for an appointment for later this week, leave the time you are looking for at the beep. Better yet, text it to me!

Thank you for calling and make today awesome.

...

Your ONE AND DONE script will be comprised of the original nine pillars:
- Your practice name and location
- Your name and title
- A warm greeting

- What information this message will provide and how to bypass it
- Address each type of caller (new clients, current clients, clients coming back)
- Your website
- Your regular hours
- The best way to get the information they need
- A warm exit

PEN TO PAPER
one and done

Your practice name and location:

Your name and title:

A warm greeting:

What information this message will provide, how to bypass it:

Address what new people should do:

Address what current clients should do:

Address what people coming back should do:

Your website:

Your regular hours:

The best way to get them what they need ASAP:

A warm exit:

There you have it. The right funnels for the right solutions. Now, let's talk texting.

Texting is a practice game changer.

Before I get into the greatest gift I am going to spark for you, I want to remind you that to successfully go staffless, you need to be your own best friend. You need to set yourself up to stay out of overwhelm, and avoid chaos at all costs.

Here is the deal — you really can get all things to all people in a matter of seconds with the right texting program. I run a very busy family wellness practice and I do it without staff. The caveat to running a staffless practice is that situations come up where things need to be communicated or appointments need to be moved in a pinch.

I don't like pinches. They hurt. But they happen. And when they do, texting is the name of the game. When I need to send a quick message and get a quick reply in a matter of moments, sometimes seconds, the solution is texting.

It provides a vehicle for concise, immediate communication without having to go into a long, drawn-out conversation. If utilized correctly your texting program could very easily be the number one tool your automated practice leans on.

Please be mindful though — there are some situations which really do require a conversation or an in-person meeting. Use your discretion.

Office snapshot.

It's Tuesday afternoon and I have three people waiting for an appointment, kids playing on the floor with the train table, four clients in my treatment area, and a new client just walked in thirty minutes early for her first appointment.

It happens. I don't set it up that way, but it happens. I'm out of room and out of seats. I know I have two more people coming in another fifteen minutes, but there's nowhere for them to hang out. And in walks Sally, wanting a surprise visit. Yep. My office is full.

Give me ten seconds on any screen to shoot a pre-written text to my next round of people coming in to tell them to come ten minutes later. I have set it up so that I have a ten minute break coming up shortly. I do that for a reason, for this reason.

Done. See that? What would've been a ten minute effort with phone calls or stopping me in my tracks and disconnecting me from my practice rhythm, now takes me all of ten seconds. The right words to the right people for immediate results. I can't tell you how many times a week I put fires out or catch them before they start with my texting program.

Any screen will do.

Ideally, you can access your texts on any screen (computers, phones, etc.) but you have to find the right program to do so!

Many texting programs use a cloud for storage, which means your content and information is always accessible to you on any screen with internet access. Very similar to an inbox, the texts waiting for a response end up becoming somewhat of a to-do list for your practice.

Texting templates.

Ready for the automation two-step dance? Copy-paste, copy-paste, copy-paste. Tah-dah! Create the right responses to any situation that could come up in a pinch or a request that needs to be responded to appropriately. Create these templates when you are calm, centered, and thinking clearly.

Make your texting system as simple and automated as possible. A template is a pre-written text or email which takes seconds to insert (literally, you click a button) as a response to a request or a message that needs to go out.

Create the list of templates your practice will need. Think of the most common questions that come up about your practice, your care, your visits, your systems, etc.

You want a template for each of the following:
- Scheduling (hours, availability)
- New client process
- Fee system / insurance questions
- Location of practice
- Current promotions
- How to book online
- How to start care with you
- How to share your practice with friends and family
- Review requests
- How to book a tele-health call
- The best way to reach you
- Quick answers to comments like *got it* or *I understand* or *I will be right there.*

I am providing you with examples of creative communication with texting. Always make them your own. If these words don't resonate with you or match your practice systems, change them.

Appointment reminders:
You have a spot at PRACTICE NAME — smart move. Come in at your appt. time. Not earlier or later. If you're more than 5 minutes late, text me to see if I can still get you in. Finish with something sweet.

Invoice sent from software program:
Hey! I Just emailed you an invoice for your visit. Once you take care of it, your account will be updated. Thanks, talk soon!

New client requesting information:
Thank you for your interest in PRACTICE NAME. Our initial consult is $$$. It includes XYZ. Our per visit fee is $$$. Please reach out if you have any questions.

About insurance and fees:
Our insurance policy is XYZ. The first visit investment is $$$. Go to WEBSITE ADDRESS to learn more about our insurance program.

Link to scheduling site:
Please go to WEBSITE ADDRESS to book a time to meet with me.

First visit information:
Hi there, we'll start with *what you include on your first visit*. Here's a link to the page to get you set up: \www.yourwebsitehere.com

Current office hours:
Current hours are: abbreviate here

A few texting tips:
- When you send a website link, check to see if you need to shortcut the link. For our app, we need to insert a \ then we can put in the site address.
- Compliance - know what you are allowed to text out and what you are not allowed to text out. In my neck of the woods, you have to be really mindful of privacy regulations.

- Be honoring of the time you send texts. Don't text people before the start of business, or late at night. It's just not cool. It can wait.
- Most texting programs can send a text to your entire contact list or parts of it, while only appearing to be a one-on-one text to the receiver. There are lots of cool features like this out there. Shop around. Get the right program for your practice.

Email when more is needed.

Sometimes voicemail and texting isn't enough. Our clients need more. If we use the right words at the right times without too much or too little, we can set the stage for beautiful, lifelong relationships with our clients. On the same hand, if we neglect communication with our clients and the community we are building, it can leave us spinning in circles.

There are a lot of details that need to be addressed, agreed to, and executed when bringing a new client into your practice. Remember, they don't know you and what you do. They don't know what sets you apart from the guy down the street with the same title.

They don't know how much attention to detail you consider and how much appreciation you have for them. This is your time to show them.

New Client Emails.

Now that your voicemail system and your texting program are set and rolling, we are going to provide you with the tools to create effective, directive email communication for all of your clients. Let's start with the new ones.

These prewritten emails will live in a compliant, accessible place to easily copy and paste or set and sign with the click of a keyboard — in no time at all.

To appreciate the flow of the new client email process, it is important for you to understand my intake process (as it dictates what happens when).

Do NOT get overwhelmed here. This is ALL stuff we lead you through in SEWP School (more coming).

At the time I am writing these words, my initial consultation process involves the following steps:

1. My new people find me usually through a referral. They either call or text my office phone to book their initial consultation. Either way, through my *voicemail message funnel*, they are led to my website to book their visit.
2. I see their booked appointment, I send them EMAIL 1, (hang tight, details coming) review their history form, and collect payment.
3. We have their tele-health call. I start each tele-health call moving through a very quick admin checklist (office procedures, money confirmation, what is coming up, etc.) with my new clients. The rest of the time is allocated for me to learn about what they are looking for.

Side note: I do a lot of listening during this call, not much talking. Before we end the call, we book their first in-person meeting where we do an exam and give them their first treatment (assuming I am going to be accepting them for care).

4. I send them EMAIL 2 once they leave the office.
5. We have another tele-health call to go over findings and recommendations. They accept care, and I send them EMAIL 3.

I am suggesting that you create three emails to get your new clients successfully started with your practice:

EMAIL 1: *welcome email* confirming first visit appointment time;

EMAIL 2: *follow-up email* after your client's first meeting with you;

EMAIL 3: *welcome to the practice* email once your client accepts care.

The following steps will put the right words together to create successful new client experiences. Remember to add your personal touch here and there.

EMAIL 1 - Confirm Appointment
The first email is a welcome note confirming their first appointment as a new client. Make sure it's clear, well-written, and easy to follow.
- Express reassurance and excitement about your first meeting with them
- Go over the steps of your new client intake process
- Confirm their appointment type, time, and date
- If your office software sends reminders, give them a heads up to be on the lookout for them
- Provide contact information and directions to your practice
- Share your in-house rules on perfumes/sanitation, etc.
- Provide financial information for your intake process
- Lead them to where they can learn more about you and your work

- Let them know you appreciate their time
- Include a note about what makes you unique (include mission statement)
- Share a testimonial or two from clients with similar backgrounds, issues, or symptoms
- End on a sweet note

Answer the following to gain clarity about what you want to communicate to your clients:
How would you like to assure your new clients that they are in the right place?

What is your process for visit one and visit two?

What are your office rules regarding in-person visits? Perfumes/tardiness/noise?

What are your financial policies for your intake process?

What unique qualities or practice offerings do you want your new clients to know about before they come to see you?

If you were new in your practice, what would you want to read/see/hear before your first visit? What about before you started care?

An example of EMAIL 1 may look something like this:

Dear Sally,

I am really looking forward to meeting with you. I am sure we will figure out how I can help you reach your health goals! We are going to start with a tele-health call on DAY at TIME.

We will schedule your first in-office visit before we end your call. Your first visit to my office will be about 30 minutes and is all about making sure you are in the right place to get the care you need. We will do a detailed exam, and as long as I feel I can help, we will give you a chiropractic adjustment.

We will follow up our time together with one more tele-health call reviewing all of my findings and recommendations. That is when we will discuss timing, money, any concerns you may have, and ancillary recommendations.

My initial consultation is an investment of $$$. You will get a directive email from my software program to get all set up!

If you need anything, reach out to my office texting line at PHONE NUMBER. Please note that texting is always the best way to get in touch with me.

You can also visit us online at WEBSITE for directions, more information about my work, and anything else you may need to know. Our website has some lovely testimonials from people I have served over the years. Please take some time to indulge.

I ask that you don't wear perfume to your visit, as I have other practice members who are sensitive to it.

You have nothing to worry about in my office, you will find that my care is gentle and kind, and my hope is that you love your experience with me.

Here is what one of my long-time clients had to say about my care:

Dr. Jodi has helped me in ways beyond my expectations. She is the real deal. I don't know how she does what she does, but I sure am glad me and my family found her! We are clients for life!
Jocelyn Brown, 2020

I can't wait to serve you, Sally.
Talk soon.
Dr. Jodi

PEN TO PAPER
email one

Express reassurance and excitement about meeting with them:

Review the steps of your new client intake process:

Confirm their appointment type, time, and date:

Reminder to look for appointment reminders from software:

Contact info and directions:

Share your in-house rules on stuff like perfumes and tobacco, etc.:

Provide financial information for your intake process:

Lead them to where they can learn more about you and your work:

Let them know you appreciate their time:

Include a note about what makes you unique (include mission statement):

Share a testimonial or two from clients with similar backgrounds, issues, or symptoms:

End on a sweet note:

...

EMAIL 2 - Follow-up

This email serves as a follow-up email after you meet with your new clients, to provide them with the following:

- Reassurance that you enjoyed your meeting with them
- Instructions on what happens next
- Your report of findings and details about reviewing it with you
- Any financial details you need to present regarding their care
- A reminder about preliminary recommendations that you made during your first visit
- Reassurance that they have found the right practice to help them

- A link to where they can see your reviews/ testimonials
- If you want to go the extra mile, you can record a personalized welcome video with details
- A sweet exit

Start with exploring the following questions:
How do you want to celebrate and/or communicate your appreciation for your new clients?

What do you want to include in your report of findings with your new clients?

What happens after your first visit?

What financial details need to be communicated about your practice with a new client?

What are common ancillary recommendations you have for new clients?

Side note: It will save you a ton of time to have all of your recommendations listed in your template, then delete the ones not relevant to this specific client. Include hyperlinks to sites that are relevant.

Do you currently have an online location for testimonials from current clients? If not, what needs to be done to create one?

An example of EMAIL 2 may look something like this:

Sally, it was great to meet with you! I really enjoyed getting to know you and I am really looking forward to serving you with great care. We are going to have one more tele-health call together to go over my findings, you can book that HERE (hyperlink).

You were sent a report with all of my findings, notes, and recommendations. Please let me know if you did not receive it.

HERE is a link to a financial plan that will work best for the care plan I am suggesting (hyperlink). Please remember, I would like to see you get started with a daily walk. Today! Thirty minutes a day is a great start.

I am certain that our care together will create ease for you and address so much of what we talked about, and I am really excited to get started.
Dr. Jodi

PEN TO PAPER
email two

Reassurance that you enjoyed your meeting with them and they have found the right practitioner:

Instructions on what happens next:

Your report of findings and details about reviewing it with you:

Any financial details you need to present regarding their care:

A reminder about preliminary recommendations that you have made during your first visit:

Provide a link to where they can see your reviews/ testimonials:

If you want to go the extra mile, record a personalized welcome video with details:

A sweet exit:

...

EMAIL 3 - Welcome

They have accepted care with you, now it is time to welcome them to the practice with EMAIL 3. It should include the following:

- A warm welcome to the practice
- Tips on how to get the most out of their care
- Scheduling and admin reminders
- Programs and systems your clients will become familiar with
- Staffless practice details
- Family care offer
- What they can expect from here
- A warm exit

Explore a bit with the following questions before writing out EMAIL 3:
How do you want to officially welcome new clients to your practice?

Is it different from their first welcome email now that they are a member of the practice?

What do your clients need to know to get the most out of their care?

What are your policies regarding your schedule?

Administrative needs?

What programs or systems will your clients become familiar with during their time at your practice? What do you want to say about them? Do you need to provide tutorials? Passwords?

What do your clients need to know about your staff? Or lack of staff?

Do you make any offers for family care to new clients? To friends of new clients?

What can your new clients expect once they join your practice?

Do you want to offer to send your report (in compliant ways) to other health care providers?

Here is an example of EMAIL 3 for new clients:
Dear Sally!
Welcome to LightSource Chiropractic! You are officially a member of my practice! Congratulations on taking a great step forward in your healthcare regime!

Please remember - I want to see you working out a few times a week and drinking a lot of water. We also spoke about letting go of sugar during your first month of chiropractic care. Be sure to keep me posted about how all of this goes.

Just a reminder that we use THIS PROGRAM for scheduling appointments (hyperlink). You should be all set to go with your first round of appointments per our tele-health call.

Remember Sally, I am a one-woman show, and you will get your administrative needs addressed as quickly as possible by texting me.

If you ever feel that I drop the ball with any part of your admin care, please bring it to my attention immediately. My goal is to far exceed your expectations every time.

If you have any family members at home who would like to come in and go through the process that you just completed with me, please let me know.

From here you can expect the best in chiropractic care each time you are at my office, and you will be treated like family.

Please make use of our lending library, our snack area, and always take the opportunity to chitchat with other moms waiting for their appointments. Our practice is made up of the coolest people around!

Welcome!
I can't wait to serve you.
Dr. Jodi

PEN TO PAPER
email three

A warm welcome to the practice:

Tips on how to get the most out of their care:

Scheduling and admin reminders:

Programs and systems your clients will become familiar with:

Staffless practice details:

Family care offer:

A warm exit:

...

Look at that! You did it! You have got the words for the people to get the information they need. Take a moment, pat yourself on the back. Now onto email campaigns. This is good stuff.

Email campaigns.

I am very passionate about my work. I feel it is my responsibility to educate so that my clients are not only healthier from their dance with me, but also more empowered. I empower through education. I share the facts, research, strategies, experience, and hope that I have gained over the years, with each new client I serve.

I'm no fool. I know that some of my clients will never read the emails I send them. In fact, the fancy system through which I send my emails shows me who opens what emails, along with the statistics of each engagement. Really cool.

I am clear that my role in the initial consultation process is to educate and provide solutions. I do a great deal of this communicating in email.

Create your email campaigns to ensure optimal communication with your new, current, and long- lost clients. As always, be sure to personalize them, making them yours with your personal flare.

In this next section we are going to review *New Client Email Campaigns* and *Inactive Client Email Campaigns*.

You can also create campaigns for alliance partners, educators, consumers of products that you may offer, and so much more! There is a TON of information waiting for you on this in SEWP School. Hang tight.

You need a software program that is going to do most of the email campaign's work for you. If you set it up right, all you should have to do is enter your client's information, set them up on the right campaign, and *voila*! They are set to go!

Remember, you want to be compliant with all of this! Find out what your local and regional legalities are concerning emails and privacy for your clients. This is really, really important!

Your email campaign should be set up for sending out specific emails on specifically numbered days. There are many choices in software programs that will do this, and do it well. You want the ability to see analytics of each campaign (how many people are opening your emails and when they open them).

Ideally you can set up the day number for sending each email in the campaign. It would be great to find a program that also integrates other components of client care like saved replies, texting, landing pages, to-do lists for each client file, etc.

The New Client Email Campaign.

Once your new clients accept care, we want to make sure they get a sequence of emails that educates them, nourishes them with great information, and nurtures their relationship with you and your office.

We are going to put together a twelve-week email campaign for your new clients. Feel free to take it further if it suits you and your practice needs.

Start with the following questions:
Are there practice systems that you want to share with your new clients?

Do you want to share what is special about your office and your care? Your training?

Are there any practice philosophies that you want to share with your new clients?

Do you want to provide your new clients with a bit of your story and background? Perhaps how you got into the work that you do?

If you were a new member of your practice, new to your policies, philosophy, understanding of the ways of the world (in relation to your care), what links would you want access to?

What organizations would you want to be introduced to?

Is there suggested reading that could benefit your new clients that you could include?

Are there any videos or films that would be helpful to learn more about you and your craft. Perhaps you recording a video or two about your care?

What email would you want to receive to make you feel welcomed as a member of the practice?

EMAIL FOR WEEK 1
Remember, your new clients may be overwhelmed, exhausted, and still digesting the concept of working with you. Don't give them too much.

Perhaps include a reminder about scheduling guidelines along with a reminder to join your social media channels. This would also be a good place to give them pointers regarding specific practice systems and procedures.

Some topics to include in your WEEK 1 email:
- Celebrate their commitment to care
- Reconfirm your promise to them
- Give them your details again (text line, best form of communication, email address, etc.)
- Introduce them to your Social Media channels
- Remind them of any scheduling guidelines

WEEK 1 email sample:
Sally,

I wanted to reach out and let you know we're thrilled to walk this journey with you. We realize you have a choice in health care providers, and I humbly thank you for choosing me! Please let me know if you have any questions along the way. We're here to serve you!

As a member of our chiropractic family, you will be loved on, treasured, and treated with respect. I can't wait to show you how we roll!

Remember, the best way to get us quickly is through our texting program at XXX-XXX-XXXX.

Please save this number to your cell phone!
Talk soon!
Dr. Jodi

EMAIL FOR WEEK 2

Your clients are getting situated by now and used to weaving your care into their weekly routine.

They can probably take some education on at this point. Don't overdo it. Just a piece or two about how important your care is and what they should be expecting.

This is also a great time to share what is available to them as a member of your practice — perhaps products you sell that support your care or some other services you offer.

Some topics to include in your WEEK 2 email:
- A heartfelt check-in
- Introduction to ancillary services or products
- Reminder to join your social media group(s)

Sample of WEEK 2 email:
Hey there Sally,
You good?
I sure do love having you around the office.
I trust you are feeling comfortable with your process and settled in as a member of the practice!

I'm a plant medicine enthusiast and have been for over 25 years! I have used essential oils through grad school, practice setup, and pregnancies, with THOUSANDS of clients, my kids, and my home care. I LOVE to share all OILS with my clients. Chances are we have already had a chat about them and how I want to see you implement them and for what.

If you want to DIVE IN and spend some time with me creating a customized order JUST FOR YOU, click HERE (hyperlink) and we will get that rolling. OILY TOOLS ROCK! And yes, the company I order from has a TON of resources besides oils: supplements, skin care, home care and more!

Oh, and if you have not yet done so, please join our practice Facebook group HERE.

Loving you from here,
Dr. Jodi

EMAIL FOR WEEKS 3 AND 4

By now your new clients are well on their way to knowing you and your systems, and perhaps experiencing some results from your care.

Send them an educational piece about what they can continue to expect from your care. Include reassurance about their process. If you run a family wellness practice, this is a great time to remind them of that and that you have room in your schedule to meet with family members who may be ready for your care.

Topic to include in WEEK 3 AND 4 emails:
- Educational pieces about progress and your care
- What to be expecting at this point of care
- Some testimonials from other clients
- A reminder that you do offer family care
- An offer for a family referral

Sample of WEEKS 3 AND 4 email:
Hey there Sally, how's it going?

Everybody reacts to adjustments differently! We want to make sure to honor the experience your body is having as a result of having a healthier nerve system.

You may experience increased range of motion, less intense pain or less frequency of pain. Clients have even described feeling a surge of energy.

Also, just a reminder, I'm always happy to speak with you directly if you have an urgent need or want to share with me in private! You can always text xxx-xxx-xxxx for support.

Is there anyone at home who should be getting adjusted too? If so, have them shoot me a text and I will get them on the schedule.

Loving you from here,
Dr. Jodi

EMAIL FOR WEEKS 5 AND 6

Your people are loving your care by now and get what you do, how big of an impact it makes, etc. Let's throw in some more education, and ask for some lovin', shall we?

Include a reference or two for them to learn more about what you do, a copy of your mission statement, and perhaps a personal story about your experience in practice. This is also a good time to ask for an online review request or testimonial request.

Include in your WEEKS 5 AND 6 email:
- Check-in for any questions they may have
- Another educational piece

- A personal story about you
- A reminder of your practice mission statement
- A testimonial request

Sample of WEEKS 5 AND 6 email:

Hey there Sally,

Wow! Is it really a month and a half that you have been with the practice? Time flies! How are you doing? Do you have any questions for me?

Remember, your nerve system controls and coordinates everything you do, and we are getting it healthier through great chiropractic care!

I am really enjoying being your chiropractor and want to make sure if there is anyone at home interested in our care, we give them the attention they deserve. Please let me know if you want me to set some time aside in the next couple of weeks for them.

This is also a great time for us to share what you are getting out of chiropractic with your friends and family! Remember, many people start their chiropractic care because they heard about how awesome it is from someone who loves them! So, who do you love who needs some great care? Share our office information with them, please!

I love being your Chiropractor, and I am so glad you chose me.
Dr. Jodi

EMAIL FOR DAY 90

By day 90, our new clients may be ready for a re-evaluation — time to check in and make sure that you are meeting their expectations and setting the stage for the next phase of care.

This email is going to provide:
• Re-evaluation process outline
• Reason for re-evaluation
• One-click solution for re-evaluation set-up

Sample of the DAY 90 email:

Hey Sally,

Every few months we review your care plan, do another exam, compare this exam to your first exam, and ensure we are meeting your expectations. I want to ensure you are moving at a pace you're happy with. I also want to double-click on our plan from here.

Let's get started with your re-evaluation. If you have not scheduled it yet, you can do so here (hyperlink). I am really looking forward to celebrating your progress with you.

Dr. Jodi

...

Make your new client email campaign your own. So that would be my email campaign. I do me. You do you. You may find that there are certain parts of this campaign I have laid out that just don't resonate with you and your practice flow. Totally cool, make it your own!

Here are some more probing questions to move you along, now that you have seen a campaign in action:

What are the top five questions that come up with your clients (over and over), regarding your care?

Your practice?

What questions would you have if you were your practice member?

What would you want to know more about?

What do you want/need to teach your clients about that you are not teaching them about now?

What resources/links do you want to include in your education to your clients?

How often would you want to get a content-based email during your first year in a new practice or community?

What would you want to see in it?

What products do you want to share with your new clients in your new client campaign? Services? Websites? Organizations?

...

Ok, good job. You've got it. Next.

Inactivation Email Campaign.

Ok, listen up. People will leave your practice. Some will move, some will feel that they have graduated from your care, some will switch to the guy down the street. It's just the way the cookie crumbles. It is not about you, ever! It is about them and their journey.

With that being said, we don't want clients who decide to leave our practice to forget that we're here for them! Even if they hear from us once every couple of months, it's still important to continue communication.

Communicate in style — not too much, not too little. You will notice that my suggested pace of emails is once every couple of months. More than that may be too much, but as always, use your discretion.

You also want to be sure to update your emails regularly, making sure they remain relevant to your current practice systems. Set a reminder for every few months to revisit your campaigns and update accordingly.

The following are concepts to follow for each email of your Inactivation Email Campaign:

Month 1
Let them know they're missed at the office. Give them a few words about why regular care is important.

Month 3
Send them a photo of a client with a testimonial. Give them an offer to reconnect with your care.

Month 5
Send them a research reference on your work and why it is important. Tell them one fun story about an interaction with a client.

Month 7
Send them a personal letter about why you love what you do. Include a copy of your mission statement or practice purpose statement.

Month 9
Share with them how your work can serve different types of people. Include a few testimonials that are relevant to your message.

Month 11

Send them a photo of a client with a testimonial (always get permission first). Give them an offer to reconnect with your care. Let them know this is the last email they'll get from you.

Explore the following questions to further develop your Inactive Email Campaign:

What would you want to know to still feel connected to a practitioner when you leave a practice or finish care, to possibly come back in the future?

What are the top five reasons people leave your practice? These are going to be the points you address in this campaign.

What resources/links do you want to include in your education to your clients once they have left your practice?

How often would you want to get a content-based email after you left a practice or community? What would you want to see in it?

What updates/information about your services and products do you want to keep your inactive clients in the loop about?

What do you want to include in every communication with your inactive clients?

In each email that goes out, what do you want to ask your inactive clients for? About? How do you want to receive their responses?

Ok, you have the tools, now create your inactive client campaign and set it in motion. This will ensure that the people you have cared for who have left your practice, continue to be nurtured by you for as long as your campaign sees fit!

4
ORGANIZE YOUR TIME, MONEY & TASKS

Organization is my jam. I could organize all day long. I get that I am unique. In fact, many practitioners who are really good at what they do seriously struggle with organization.

Here's the deal — if you can organize your time and start using checklists to organize your life and practice, you can build just about anything. The sky will truly become your limit.

Take these pieces and run with them. Run far and run fast. They are key to keeping your practice and life balanced and successful.

The disorganized attorney.

When I was 30 years old, I was ready to buy my first piece of real estate. I was super nervous and I had no idea what I was getting myself into. It was time to hire my first attorney.

The pickings were slim. I live in a small town where everybody knows everybody. I had two choices — either the old school attorney who did things by the book and took his time to get back to you, or the sharky guy down the street.

I wanted this real-estate transaction to be as drama-free as possible, so I chose the old-school guy. His name was Mike.

I remember like it was yesterday (it was about 20 years ago now), walking into his office for the first time, and feeling a bit set back from what I saw. He had stacks of paper from floor to ceiling, he didn't have anybody working for him, his office definitely had a funk about it — like it hadn't had a good cleaning in months, maybe even years. Mike was, hands down, the antithesis of organized.

He was in complete chaos. His office was a mess, and he was always in a tizzy. Don't get me started on the updates needed around his space. His toilet didn't flush so I never used it (I learned my lesson the first time I tried), his phone rang so loud that I would continue to hear it for five minutes after he picked it up. And yes, he picked it up all the time while I, his client, was sitting in front of him. Really? It was all cute, until it wasn't.

At this time, all the other attorneys were starting to fax through email and from their smartphones (only really fancy people like attorneys had smartphones). That seemed like a really big deal to me.

I didn't mind that Mike was behind the times. In fact, I really liked him. He had a father feel about him that made me feel safe, and safety was something that I really needed with this huge transaction.

I trusted that he could get the job done. He had a passion for the law that resembled my love for chiropractic. His law books were well loved on, dusty and dirty, filled with dog-eared pages. He would tell law stories as if he were talking about his own kids.

I really admired a lot about his old-school ways; however, they were becoming an obstacle to getting what I really wanted as his client. His disorganization got in the way.

I remember thinking to myself if he actually took time to make some of the stuff work quicker and smoother, how much more graceful my journey with him could have been.

It all worked out in the long run. I got the building. He did his job. I did my job and life went on. However, with a little updating, and a touch of automation, Mike could have been so much more efficient, and my experience as his client that much better.

Organization & overwhelm.

Okay, onto organization. First, get out of overwhelm. Overwhelm sucks. It can make or break your experience. We move through the world wearing a lot of hats, and we want to make sure that under those hats you have a peaceful, happy mind. Get out of overwhelm friend, and watch your world change!

Take a minute to review the last 24 hours. How many situations did you react to as opposed to respond to?

How many important tasks did you forget? What moving pieces of your busy life did you misguide due to your current state of overwhelm?

It's time for change and this is just the tool to get you started. Start with free access to the BEST to-do list, ever.

The pediatrician with no time.

Dr. Jen had been working over 40 hours a week running her family wellness practice. Before she knew it, the 40 hours started to become 45, then 50. She is a pediatrician in New York City with a forever dream of running her own practice that creates a big difference in her community. However as of late, she finds herself run down, depleted, and regretting some of the decisions she has made.

Dr. Jen has two kids and a husband who is battling chronic Lyme disease. He has it under control, but it is another thing that she has on her mind.

Dr. Jen has spent thousands of dollars, and even more hours, studying and training to get this process right.

Yet she still feels like no matter what she does, the challenge of balancing work/home life and not running out of time keeps her up at night.

She found Staffless Practice through a friend and decided to grab a seat to SEWP School. A few months after her study with SEWP School began, Dr. Jen started to implement our TIME MAP TOOL.

She started with a time study, soon to recognize how much time she was spending on tasks that really could be delegated to a virtual assistant or someone in-house part time. Things that were just not the best use of her time, like filing and billing and cleaning, could easily go to an assistant.

She realized how little time she was spending doing fun things that used to bring her joy, like playing with her kids and crafting with her girlfriends.

She got away from going to the gym, and it is affecting how she is feeling about herself.

Little by little, one change at a time, Dr. Jen started to make changes. She began to feel the balance seep into her life. The more she created and implemented the right systems, the more she got back to practicing and living the way that she wanted to.

These days, Dr. Jen keeps her practice light and fun, filled with her ideal clients and systems that work for her. She has a part-time staff member who does the grunt work of cleaning, filing, etc. She keeps it really simple with her staff member and it works. She has a lot more time for her family and spends a lot less time at the office.

Time for a time study.

I have a very clear memory from years ago, of complaining to my coach about how frustrated I was while trying to get stains out of my office carpet. My coach stopped me in my tracks, and with all of the love in his heart simply responded to me, Jodi, is that really the best use of your time?

His words struck a chord with me — pretty deep. Deep enough that I remember them to this day. At that moment I made a commitment to only do things that are worth my time.

Furthermore, I committed to delegate the things that are not the best use of my time to someone who could do them better, smarter, and faster. I have come a long way with this stuff, and there is still room for improvement, but it is going in the right direction.

As busy practitioners, we often spend too much time on things that don't lead us to where we want to be. That needs to change, pronto! If we want to run an automated practice without staff, we need to make every practice moment count. We need to know what tasks can be dropped, what needs to be delegated, and what we need to do a bit more or less of.

Let's do a time study!

Get clear on when your time to play is, when you need to focus, when you need to be on, and when you need to disconnect. The following time study is exactly that — a study of how you currently spend your time. It will give you a 20/20 view of what you're currently doing with your time, so you can make empowering decisions and create the schedule you need to rock your practice and enjoy your life!

Start to see how much time you are wasting doing low-dollar activities, so you can start to see how much time can be saved by NOT doing them (delegation).

Don't get bogged down with the technicalities of this exercise. Guesstimate, stay flexible and have fun!

Time study directions:
- Start your time study this coming Monday.
- Record how you use your time, each activity that you do throughout the day.

- Record how much money that activity is worth, by guesstimating what you would pay someone to do it for you.
- Remember, some things you do are priceless and some are worth minimum wage. Don't think too far into this, just record.
- Once you have finished a week's worth of time study, review with the steps below.

List the activities you did this week that are valued at:
$$\$0\text{-}\$15/hr$$
$$\$20\text{-}\$50/hr$$
$$\$55\text{-}\$90/hr$$
$$\$100 +/hr$$

Reflect on:
- What patterns you recognize
- What you are currently doing with your time that you are really proud of
- What needs to change
- Things that you need to delegate
- Things that you simply need to stop doing
- Things that you need to do more of

The point of this work is not to get down on yourself or punish yourself for not being good enough. It is simply to recognize the patterns that you have with time, and change what is no longer serving you. Start there. What is no longer serving you? Remove it, and watch what happens!

The time map and it's components.

Play with me for a minute — you are in New Jersey. You want to get to California. You decide to take a few days and make it a drive. You have all good intentions - your car is set, your food is packed, your bags are in the car. But wait. No map.

No directions. No course of action. No good.

Maps are crucial to getting to where you want to go, especially when it comes to creating more time, and having a more direction organized approach to your practice and life schedule.

You are about to create a gorgeous, organized, implementable time map that will lead to direction and order for your life.

You have already done the study. You know where the gaps that need to be mended are. Maybe you have even begun to mend them. Now we create a plan — we break out the time map to give you ultimate control of the roads you travel!

Your map is made up of time signatures.
A time signature is a segment of time committed to specific intention or action or group of actions, all leading to the same outcome. Take a look at your study, and you will see that you naturally have signatures, you just need to categorize them.

Time Map Signatures:
Must Do's
These are activities that occur regularly. They are part of your routine, not likely to change any time soon. Examples: practice hours, classes, meetings, regular family obligations, etc.

Date Time
This is time with your love. If you're single, plan it with yourself. It can be an evening, afternoon, or an entire day!

Family Time
This is the time to focus on your kids, family, friends, etc. This is when you enjoy the people you love — including yourself. Parents - remember, kids are kids once. Enjoy it.

Diamond Time
This is your focused, distraction-free time. It's when you create and manifest plans for your practice. It's important not to go more than three hours straight with these hours.

We want to keep your mind and energy fresh and focused.

There can be no distractions during this time. Go to a coffee shop or library to get this done if need be. No phones or emails during this time!

Busy Time

This is the time that you're getting life done, i.e., errands, cleaning, grocery shopping, washing your car and more.

Me Time

This is time you spend with yourself, having fun, doing hobbies and self-care. This can include food prep, getting bodywork, working out, etc. This is the time you include in your schedule to take care of you.

Nothing at all Time

Not every moment needs to be scheduled! It is quite lovely to have time in your schedule for nothing at all! But most of us really do need to schedule it in!

If there are any time signatures that are relevant to your life, please add them to your time map.

Remember when creating your map:

- Make it colorful! We live in a multi-dimensional, colorful world. Your time map should represent that!
- This is a living document; you can change it at any time! As your life evolves and changes, so will your schedule.
- If during the week you have an interruption in your map, schedule the interrupted time for another spot that week.

- Be sure to revisit this regularly. Put a reminder in your schedule to check in with it every few weeks and move stuff around if needed.
- Once you complete your map and make sure it is just so, share it with the people in your life. Let them hold you accountable to maintaining it.

Create your time map.

If I follow my current time map, I am good. I can get a lot more done than if I choose to put it to the side. Sometimes I do put it aside and I regret it.

I get disorganized and overwhelmed and let things slip. The key for me and my automated practice is staying organized with my time.

All of the signatures are important for me, but the most important for me is the *nothing at all* time. I need it like I need air. I can handle doing a lot, serving a lot, being Mommy a lot, as long as I can see my *nothing at all time* on the horizon.

You will need to revisit and shape-shift your time map. Flexibility must apply here. Start with figuring out when you focus best, when you move best, when you rest best, and when you play best, then just plug and play — filling in the grids for each time signature. You may want to start with the time signatures you feel are most relevant or highest priority.

Checklists make it all happen.

Think about the moments when you have clients standing in front of you, the phone is ringing, the dog is barking, the toilet just overflowed, the kid in your waiting room spilled his goldfish crackers all over your new carpet, and you feel a migraine coming on.

Think *checklists.* If you use your checklists the way I recommend, you will better avoid these moments of Crazytown. Your practice will be thought out, well planned, and solution based.

I get asked all the time how I get everything done that I get done — and my answer is always *checklists*.

Checklists make my life possible. Period.

They make it so that I don't have to think when I'm doing 100 things with my clients and my kids and my family and my house and the car and the dog.

You know where I'm going with this. Checklists allow me to lean on the systems that I created when it was quiet and I was focused and thinking clearly (as opposed to reacting through the world and doing something in spite of what may be good for me, just to get it done and off the list).

If I don't have my checklists in front of me, on my phone, or by my desk, I tend to react according to what I am feeling in that moment, and the outcome usually sets me back or gets me in some kind of a rut.

I have checklists for office money stuff, new client processing, the initial tele-health call, re-evaluations, house chores, office supplies, weekly and monthly marketing tasks, and so much more.

If I am really on point, my checklists are combined in the perfect tickler system to remind me of what to do and when to do it for all aspects of my life.

Just about 100% of the time when something in my life is not working, I can double click on it and see that I have dropped the ball with the implementation of one of my checklists. Of course, there are exceptions to this, but most of the time it is true for me.

During the times that I have had staff working at the office, their checklists defined their job outline, became an accountability tool (they handed in their completed checklist at the end of each week), and acted as a review sheet to re-evaluate and change systems with.

I could use the checklists for each role at my office as a job outline, a check and balance sheet for their performance, and a concrete agreement of their roles and responsibilities. Remember, as their roles change, the items on the checklists change too. Everyone knows who is doing what, according to their checklists. Cool, right?

There are different types of checklists for different types of situations. I am including a few of my favorite checklists here. There are a lot more in SEWP School, but this collection will get you started. Remember to personalize these lists to work for you and your lifestyle.

In this section we will review the following:
New Client Checklist - everything you need to do from start to finish with a new client.

Re-evaluation Checklist - the steps to ensuring that your re-evaluations are thorough and successful.

Abundance Checklists - get the steps down to create, manage, and organize your practice and personal finances.

New Client Checklist.

Put yourself in the shoes of your new clients who don't know you, have a strong reason that they are seeing you, and want to have a great experience with you. What do they need to hear? See? Read? Experience? What would you want your experience to include? Here is a sample of a New Client Checklist. Study it, then make your own!

Before visit 1
☐ Enter in software program
☐ Enter in texting program
☐ Send a welcome text
☐ Categorize name in texting program
☐ Send EMAIL 1
☐ Get & review history
☐ Collect payment

At visit 1
☐ Exam notes
☐ Create care plan recommendations
☐ Schedule visit #2

After visit 1
☐ Complete demographics in software
☐ Check insurance
☐ Send EMAIL 2

At visit 2

☐ Book appointments and first re-eval

☐ Change status in texting program

☐ Send EMAIL 3

☐ Set up billing system

☐ Set reminders for re-evaluations and schedule from here

☐ Send reports to referring practitioners and other health care team members

To better personalize your new client checklist, ask yourself the following:

What are the steps that you need to take before a new client meets with you? After? Once they are a practice member?

Now, take all of the information you have compiled and create your step-by-step checklist for new client success.

Re-evaluation Checklist.

Re-evaluations are a crucial component of a successful treatment plan. They ensure we are following course with our clients and meeting the goals we set out to meet when we first put a plan together for them.

They set up accountability check-ins for us and our clients. They provide time to reconnect, course correct if needed, and get caught up with our clients. Some of the steps we include on the Re-evaluation Checklist for my practice are:

Before appointment
☐ Send a reminder email about appointment
☐ Put appointment in schedule

Review
☐ Check in on care plan goals and frequency of visits
☐ Make sure appointment reminders are being received

At appointment
☐ Ask for referrals
☐ Confirm that they're getting office emails
☐ Confirm that they're getting office texts
☐ Ask if they are a member of practice Social Media Group/Page
☐ Do exam and take notes
☐ Send reports to other practitioners on healthcare team
☐ Ask for testimonial

After appointment
☐ Update any financial agreements
☐ Update DX codes
☐ Schedule next series of appointments
☐ Schedule next re-eval

Ask yourself what you want to do for a client before and after a re-evaluation and create your own re-evaluation checklist.

Practice Abundance Checklists.

The more organization you create around money and abundance, the more room you will create for it to flow into your practice and support your life!

Take your time with this one. It will create a strong foundation for financial success!

This is an example of a weekly abundance checklist. Make it your own.

Income/expense payroll/self-pay
☐ Make bank deposit
☐ Pay bills
☐ Check money accounts
☐ Check accounts receivables - report and address issues
☐ Clean up account issues that came up throughout the week
☐ Enter and update any payment plan activity
☐ Update stats sheet

Insurance
☐ Enter insurance payments/denials
☐ Submit insurance
☐ Invoice and notify any clients with denials from insurance
☐ Check clearing house reports
☐ Check benefits
☐ Prep and submit any requests for medical notes

Personal
☐ Reading on financial health and wealth
☐ Family meeting discussions on finances
☐ See yourself in a place of abundance, bliss, and plenty

Monthly abundance lists.
There are financial tasks that don't need to be done weekly but are also crucial to keep in-check.

Here are some tasks that may nicely fit into your monthly abundance checklist:
☐ Process any memberships needed
☐ Run a new AR report
☐ Balance budget
☐ Send out invoices
☐ Check on last month's invoices to make sure they were paid
☐ Enter income and expenses in the budget
☐ Review credit card transactions and compare to what made it to the bank

Remember, these are the moving pieces that work for my abundance checklists. Study your financial picture, what needs to be done on a regular basis, and put together your own relevant checklists.

Our Academy Checklists.

Yes, I have a school for you. I know, can you handle it? And … some might refer to me as a checklist junky, and I am ok with that. So naturally, Staffless Practice Academy has an entire course on every checklist you could possibly dream of as a practitioner.

Some of our checklists that you may want to consider creating (offered in SEWP School) are:

Weekly Practice Love Checklist - what you need to remember each week to care for your practice

Forms and Supplies Checklist - forms and supplies you want to have in stock at all times

Webinar Checklist - what you need to do before, during, and after each webinar (or live event) to ensure success

Monthly Marketing Checklist - of the moving monthly pieces to a great marketing plan

So much more. Really.

5
GET MORE HELP

Discover Staffless Practice Academy.

Yep, I did. I created an entire online school with enough coaching and accountability to rest your hat on. If you have a practice, and you are coming from a wellness perspective in the ways that you serve, or the beliefs that you hold, boy- oh-boy do I have tools for you.

We field all kinds of questions from both new and seasoned practitioners, who are looking to streamline and rock their staffless practice efforts; what hours to hold, what name to use, what to do on the first visit, how to market, how to form their business, what to call their clients...the list goes on.

These are real-deal questions that deserve real-deal study. We have an entire school for you. Really...a finishing school (of sorts) that will provide you all of the lessons and tools and teachers and direction.

The Academy is an interactive, video-based training program that teaches wellness practitioners the tools they need to automate and advance their practices. There is nothing I have not thought of.

We teach practice setup, marketing strategies, client communication systems, clinical organization tools, and so much more. If there is a system or strategy that you will need for practice success, that I have not mastered (there are plenty) I have brought THE MASTERS in to teach on it.

Our goal with Staffless Practice Academy is to far exceed your expectations, and the feedback we get is that our goal is always accomplished, and then some.

The School Menu.

Our current series of courses offered in Staffless Practice Academy include the following:

REFLECT
The ultimate tools for living stress-free in practice and life.

ORGANIZE
Guides to keep all of the important components of practice in order.

SPA TRI
Create clean and clear systems for streamlining your front desk communication systems. The goal: to never answer the office phone again. Ever.

R.I.S.E.
Your one-stop-shop for creating and actualizing a rockstar, kick-ass marketing plan for your practice. Ground level tools, social media mastery, you name it.

TEACH
Create and share an online course for your community to learn and grow with your offerings.

FUNNEL
Attract, organize, and plan so you can multiply your income.

EXCHANGE
Discover balance with time, energy, and money to realize the practice and life of your dreams.

If there is a system I have not mastered, I bring in the masters to teach in my school.

Free training taste-test.

Get acquainted with my teaching style. Learn more about the awesomeness we are creating.

We have created a free training, that is sure to shape-shift your automation efforts and get you familiar with the quality of the Staffless Practice Academy experience.

Our recorded training will move you through the journey of the most common mistakes practitioners make when trying to succeed in practice and how to avoid them at all costs. It will also offer you the most current bonuses and promotions to maximize the value of our Academy School seats.

Grab our free training:
WWW.STAFFLESSPRACTICETRAINING.COM

Reach out to us.

Connection is HUGE for the Staffless Practice Community - it is FOR SURE one of our guiding core values. So, let's make this happen! Reach out, dive in, connect. We are a click of the keyboard away!

Free Facebook Community
www.facebook.com/groups/stafflesspractice

Instagram
@stafflesspractice

Website
www.joyfilledpractice.com

Free Training
www.stafflesspracticetraining.com

Speaking engagements.

I get asked to speak and share a lot, and I love it. I have a lot to share, and I make myself as available as possible! My presentation style is as exciting and entertaining as it is informative and relevant.

I for sure have a spring in my step and can dazzle a room. I can show up in a Zoom, in a room, however it works for your community. I can tailor my talks to your group's needs and current interests.

My current signature presentations are:

The Well Prepared Practitioner - Get ready to rock practice with automated solutions.

From Graduation to Lights On - New in practice? We've got you! All of the moving pieces to starting out automated.

How to Turn Your Phone into an Automated Client Directory Without Losing the Personal Experience Your Clients Expect - A review and inside tricks to the Message Funnel System.

6 Things I Was Never Told Before Opening my Practice - Probably my funniest, most relatable presentation. All about the lessons learned and experience earned from years of falling down and getting back up.

All inquiries are entertained through email, connect with us at hello@joyfilledpractice.com.

I recognize that you could have spent your time with any book out there, and I am forever grateful that you chose this one. I hope you loved these concepts much as I do.

Made in the USA
Monee, IL
06 September 2023

42245033R00089